Guidelines

KW-334-409

VOL 21 / PART 1   January–April 2005

Edited by **Jeremy Duff and Katharine Dell**

Suggestions for using *Guidelines*

Set aside a regular time and place, if possible, when you can read and pray undisturbed. Before you begin, take time to be still and, if you find it helpful, use the BRF prayer.

In *Guidelines*, the introductory section provides context for the passages or themes to be studied, while the units of comment can be used daily, weekly, or whatever best fits your timetable. You will need a Bible (more than one if you want to compare different translations) as Bible passages are not included. At the end of each week is a 'Guidelines' section, offering further thoughts about, or practical application of what you have been studying.

You may find it helpful to keep a journal to record your thoughts about your study, or to note items for prayer. Another way of using *Guidelines* is to meet with others to discuss the material, either regularly or occasionally.

Occasionally, you may read something in *Guidelines* that you find particularly challenging, even uncomfortable. This is inevitable in a series of notes which draws on a wide spectrum of contributors, and doesn't believe in ducking difficult issues. Indeed, we believe that *Guidelines* readers much prefer thought-provoking material to a bland diet that only confirms what they already think.

If you do disagree with a contributor, you may find it helpful to go through these three steps. First, think about why you feel uncomfortable. Perhaps this is an idea that is new to you, or you are not happy at the way something has been expressed. Or there may be something more substantial—you may feel that the writer is guilty of sweeping generalization, factual error, theological or ethical misjudgment. Second, pray that God would use this disagreement to teach you more about his word and about yourself. Third, think about what you will do as a result of the disagreement. You might resolve to find out more about the issue, or write to the contributor or the editors of *Guidelines*. After all, we aim to be 'doers of the word', not just people who hold opinions about it.

Writers in this issue

David Wenham is the Dean of Wycliffe Hall, Oxford, and an Anglican priest. He is the author of many books on Jesus, most recently *Paul and Jesus: the True Story* (SPCK, 2002) and (with Steve Walton) *Exploring the New Testament* (SPCK, 2001).

Walter Moberly is an ordained Anglican and a Reader in Theology at the University of Durham. He is married to Jenny, who is also ordained, and the the struggling-to-keep-up father of John-Paul (10) and Rachel (5). When not indulging the pleasures of reading, he likes to savour with Jenny the countryside, history and pubs of the north-east of England.

Katharine Dell is Senior Lecturer in the Faculty of Divinity at Cambridge University and Director of Studies in Theology at St Catherine's College. She is the author of the volume on Job in BRF's *People's Bible Commentary* series.

Jeremy Duff is a member of the Theology Faculty of Oxford University. He specializes in New Testament and Ministerial Training in his roles as Tutor at Wycliffe Hall, Oxford, and Officer for Ordained Local Ministry (Education) in Liverpool Diocese.

Jill Middlemas is the Liddon Research Fellow in Theology, Keble College, Oxford, and the Hebrew Lector for the Oxford Centre for Hebrew and Jewish Studies. She is currently revising for publication (with OUP) her DPhil thesis on the inhabitants of the land during the period of the exile, entitled *The Troubles of Templeless Judah*.

Stephen Kuhrt is curate at Christ Church, New Malden. Prior to ordination he was a history teacher.

Brian Mastin was Senior Lecturer in Hebrew at the University of Wales, Bangor, before retiring to Cambridge. He is a specialist on the book of Daniel.

Rob Merchant is a self-supporting curate at St John's Church, Harborne, in Birmingham. He is currently helping to develop an educational network around dementia care and continuing part-time PhD studies looking at ageing, religion and health in the life of the older person.

Further BRF reading for this issue

For more in-depth coverage of some of the passages in these Bible reading notes, we recommend the following titles:

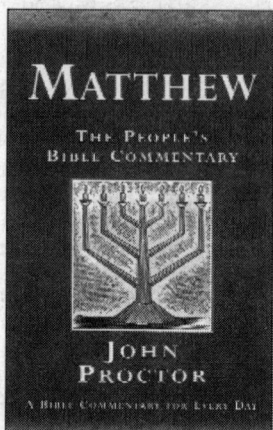

MATTHEW

THE PEOPLE'S BIBLE COMMENTARY

JOHN PROCTOR

A BIBLE COMMENTARY FOR EVERY DAY

1 84101 191 6, £7.99

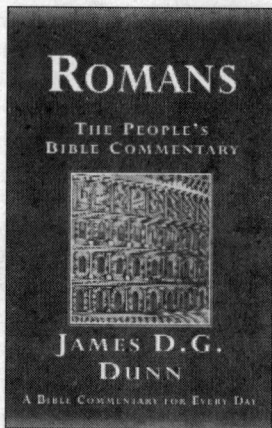

ROMANS

THE PEOPLE'S BIBLE COMMENTARY

JAMES D.G. DUNN

A BIBLE COMMENTARY FOR EVERY DAY

1 84101 082 0, £7.99

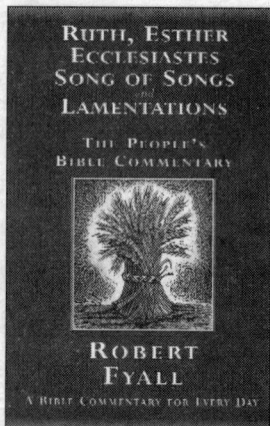

RUTH, ESTHER ECCLESIASTES SONG OF SONGS and LAMENTATIONS

THE PEOPLE'S BIBLE COMMENTARY

ROBERT FYALL

A BIBLE COMMENTARY FOR EVERY DAY

1 84101 242 4, £8.99 (available Feb 2005)

The Editors write...

The Bible contains a wealth of different types of material, testimony to how the living God speaks in many different ways, just as he calls all sorts of different people and they live through different circumstances. This issue of *Guidelines* encompasses something of this variety.

We begin with the Gospels, as we finish our study of Matthew's Gospel with David Wenham as our guide. Then we move to Old Testament narrative, continuing our theme of different characters in the Old Testament, featuring Abraham, the founder of Israel, a key figure in three world faiths—Judaism, Christianity and Islam. This study is contributed by Walter Moberly from Durham University, who has a specialist interest in these Genesis texts. Then to poetry when, coinciding with the week of St Valentine's Day, we have a one-week offering on the Song of Songs from our Old Testament editor, Katharine Dell.

From here we go to something rather different, as our New Testament editor, Jeremy Duff, leads us through the second part of Paul's letter to the Romans, which does have its poetic sections but on the whole is full of detailed argument—a letter for a particular place at a particular time. Next we have another text written in response to a particular event—the book of Lamentations—although from another point of view it is more similar to the Song of Songs, since both are great works of poetry. Jill Middlemas from Oxford explores the depths of despair found in this short book in the wider context of the genre of lament and its place in our own lives.

We approach Easter with Stephen Kuhrt, a parish priest, who invites us to look at the Easter story through the lens of Jesus' kingship, giving a different perspective to familiar New Testament texts. After Easter we plunge into the book of Daniel, the only apocalyptic writing in the Old Testament, which raises many questions in its use of fantastic imagery. These notes are presented by Brian Mastin, who is an expert on this fascinating and intriguing book. Finally, if all that has not been sufficiently challenging, we turn to the subject of old age. Rob Merchant, a specialist in religion and the older person, helps us begin to consider this significant but often overlooked or marginalized section of our population, and indeed of our own lives. Overall, a banquet of many different courses, which we hope you will enjoy.

Katharine Dell, Jeremy Duff

The BRF Prayer

Almighty God,
you have taught us that your word is a lamp for our
feet and a light for our path. Help us, and all who
prayerfully read your word, to deepen our
fellowship with each other through your love.
And in so doing may we come to know you more
fully, love you more truly, and follow more faithfully
in the steps of your son Jesus Christ, who lives and
reigns with you and the Holy Spirit,
one God for evermore. Amen.

MATTHEW 20—28

We begin the year with the final instalment in our study of Matthew's Gospel. Over the next four weeks we will consider the final nine chapters, picking up the story as Jesus is about to enter Jerusalem. Here the story turns darker: much of the teaching reflects a conflict between Jesus and other religious groups or authorities, as they try to trick him and he challenges them. The crowds begin with a positive acclamation of Jesus, similar to what we have seen in the previous chapters, but it turns sour. The future Jesus predicts for himself and for his followers is characterized by struggle and endurance. Despite this, or even because of it, the truth of God's generosity, love for the lost and oppressed, and saving power is revealed.

Quotations are taken from the New International Version of the Bible.

3–9 JANUARY

Matthew 20—22

1 God's generosity

Matthew 20:1–16

'It's not fair.' Children say it; workers say it; most of us say it or feel it from time to time. In Jesus' parable, the labourers who started work in the vineyard first thing in the morning and worked a twelve-hour day said it. They said it when the owner of the vineyard paid them exactly the same as the labourers who joined them at the eleventh hour.

Day labourers were an important part of the Palestinian economy. They were typically a poor group with no job security, and they would gather at known meeting places, hoping to pick up work. It was, obviously, ideal to get work for the whole day; a 'denarius' was a day's wage. But you had to make do with whatever you could get, and in Jesus' story some people got no work until the eleventh hour, when the owner of the vineyard saw them, spoke to them and, hearing that they had had no work all day, sent them into his vineyard. We might think it a bit of a waste of effort sending them to work for one hour, but it becomes clear that the master is acting out of compassion and generosity. Indeed, he is so generous that he pays them the full day's wage of one denarius.

We can imagine the joy when they got home and told the family what had happened, but we don't have to imagine how the other workers felt: 'It's not fair,' they say to their generous employer. He completely rejects their complaint. He has been totally fair with those who worked all day, paying them the agreed amount. The only 'problem' is his generosity to others! And that is not a problem, except to the envious complainers.

This story of Jesus comes immediately after Jesus' promises to Peter about all that God will give to his disciples: they will be greatly rewarded. God's rewards are not dished out on a reasonable pay-as-you-earn basis, however; they come out of an unreasonably kind generosity. In fact, one difference between the parable and real life is that none of us deserves God's kindness, not even Peter. All of us are recipients of undeserved love (that is, grace), and that grace is as strong towards those who come in at the eleventh hour (whose need is indeed even greater than the others') as to those who have the security of being in the Lord's employment from the beginning of the day. The only problem is the danger of envy. In the story, those who were hired at the eleventh hour got paid first, even before those who had worked longer: the last are first. It is as though the master wants the other workers to see and to learn from his generosity. Those of us who have known God's grace for a long time should be thankful when others find it, even at the end of the day, and should seek to reflect the master's enthusiastic compassion and generosity.

2 Ambition

Matthew 20:17–34

Jesus' sense of calling to self-sacrificial suffering contrasts with the selfish ambition of his followers. It is intriguing that in Matthew's Gospel it is the mother of James and John who requests top seats for her sons in Jesus' cabinet; did they realize that it was not quite the thing to ask Jesus? Did they ask their mother to be their front man (woman!)? Or was it just that she was a typically ambitious mother who wanted to make sure that they got on in life? It did not seem an unreasonable request, since James and John were among the inner three of Jesus' disciples who were at the Transfiguration and who would be there in Gethsemane.

That was the problem, however. Jesus was heading for Gethsemane and for suffering, not for a *coup d'état* against the Romans, so Jesus asks James and John (mother has retreated into the background) whether they can 'drink the cup I am going to drink'. The thought here is of a cup of suffering (not of celebration, as in Psalm 23:5). In the Old Testament, God's judgment is sometimes described as a cup—a cup of poison (Isaiah 51:17), and Jesus knew that he was going to suffer, indeed to experience the judgment of God on behalf of others. So he asks the ambitious brothers if they are up for that. They say 'yes', but in fact they will run away when Jesus is arrested (26:56).

Jesus goes on to comment on his disciples' ambitiousness, and says how ordinarily human it is. Human leaders love position and power: it is one of the greatest dangers in political and church life. Jesus calls his followers to a thoroughly counter-cultural style of leadership—being servant and slave to others. This was Jesus' own way: he came 'to serve and to give his life a ransom for many' (v. 28) In using those words, Jesus was recalling Isaiah 52 and 53, chapters that speak of God ransoming or redeeming his people from slavery in exile and of God's 'servant' bearing the sins of 'many' (53:11, 12). The thought is of God's people being punished for their sins and of the Suffering Servant of the Lord taking their judgment on himself, so that they may go free. Jesus saw himself as that servant, drinking the cup of judgment for us.

This was the model of leadership that he set before his disciples. It was a message that his followers did eventually take to heart—see Paul in 1 Corinthians 9:19: 'I make myself a slave to everyone'—but it is one that the church has very frequently forgotten since then.

3 Jesus inspects the temple

Matthew 21:1–22

It was several days' journey from Galilee to Jerusalem, and that was if you did not get delayed on the way. Jewish pilgrims did not usually take the direct route through Samaria because of the bad relations between the Jews and the Samaritans, which could turn violent (Luke 9:51–56), so they would go east across the Jordan river, then south along the river, and then turn west via Jericho and up to Jerusalem. The last stretch of the journey was especially arduous: Jericho is down in the rift valley, 770 feet below sea level; Jerusalem is only 17 miles away, but is more than 2,500 feet above sea level. It is a steep climb, and the road was famously dangerous, so when you got to the top of the Mount of Olives and saw Jerusalem just below you, it was a great feeling of relief, achievement and excitement, not least because the Passover feast was such a big and significant festival with perhaps 100,000 people converging on the city for a week.

Jesus' disciples knew that Jesus was expecting something momentous to happen, and when he asked them to find him a donkey (with its colt, according to Matthew) on which to ride into the city, they put two and two together and welcomed Jesus as king of Jerusalem. They had hoped he would become king, and now he seemed to be fulfilling the prophecy of Zechariah about the king coming on a donkey (9:9). A previous ruler, Judas Maccabeus, who had led the Jews in a successful revolt against the then ruling colonial power, had been welcomed by people cutting branches and spreading them on the road.

Jesus did not march in and drive the Romans out, however. Instead, he went to the temple area and drove out those buying and selling and doing temple business: they had, according to Jesus, turned what should have been 'a house of prayer' into a 'den of robbers' (v. 13). Jesus quoted those words from Isaiah 56:7 and Jeremiah 7:11, and thus identified himself with the Old Testament prophets who denounced the people for the emptiness of their religiosity.

It seems likely that Jesus' cursing of the fig tree (v. 19) is an acted parable continuing the same theme, warning of judgment to come on Israel for its religious fruitlessness. Jesus' religion, by contrast, was wonderfully fruitful, bringing healing, evoking the praise of God from children in the temple and offering power in response to the prayer of faith.

Jesus' followers wanted earthly power and political victory. Jesus wanted spiritual power and faithfulness. How would he rate our religion? What things might he turn over and drive out?

4 Who is obeying God?

The temple authorities were hopping mad with Jesus' violent action in the temple, and asked him to justify himself. Who had given him the authority to do these things? Jesus' counter-question about John the Baptist's authority put them on the spot: if they said John was from God, then they condemned themselves for not believing in him; if they denied that John was from God, then they feared the crowd's reaction, since John had been very popular. In posing his question, Jesus was both beating them at their own game of tricky questions and making a point about his own authority. As we have seen, he had been publicly commissioned by God for his ministry at his baptism: what happened on that occasion was an endorsement of both John and Jesus.

Jesus then goes on to the offensive with two parables, the first about the people's reaction to John the Baptist, the second about their response to Jesus himself. Jesus' first parable about two boys, one rebellious but then obedient, the other apparently obedient to his father but then rebellious, describes for Jesus the religious authorities whose apparent piety was contradicted by their failure to respond to John's call to righteousness, and contrasts them with the tax collectors and prostitutes who were obviously impious but who then believed and 'entered the kingdom of God' (v. 31).

Jesus' second parable pictures a common enough situation in first-century Palestine—an absentee landlord with a vineyard being managed by tenants. Their resentment of the master's demands for his fruit would have been familiar enough, and their violence towards his servants would not have been surprising, but their decision to kill the master's son and claim the vineyard for themselves was high-risk and most unwise, leading to the master's intervention and their loss of the tenancy and their own lives.

The parable is a pointed one, and the religious authorities recognize Jesus as saying again that they face the judgment of God for their unfruitfulness, most of all because of their rejection of Jesus, the son. His death will lead to their being 'crushed' (v. 44), and to his being vindicated. The picture used for his vindication (borrowed from Psalm

118:22) is that of a stone which is first cast out as useless by a team of builders, but which is later retrieved to become the keystone holding the building together. Jesus was cast to one side by the Jewish authorities but raised from the dead by God, that 'at the name of Jesus every knee should bow' (Philippians 2:10).

The religious authorities wanted to do their own thing and did not want to bow to God's messenger, John the Baptist, or to his Son, Jesus. Trying to take over from God is something that human beings often attempt, but it is fatal. It is in God's service that there is perfect freedom, not in rebelling against him.

5 Rejecting the king

Matthew 22:1–14

If we had some sympathy yesterday with the tenants wanting the produce of the vineyard for themselves, today's parable leaves no room for sympathy. To snub an invitation from the king to his son's wedding, because 'I'm busy with other things', was outrageous; to kill the messengers bringing the good invitation was inexcusable. The king had a right to be furious and to punish the ungrateful murderers. Jesus had previously compared his coming to a wedding (9:15). Now his warning to the religious leaders of his day, who refused his invitation to the kingdom of God, is clear; they were planning to kill the son, not to celebrate with him.

Jesus warns that they will be punished but that the banquet will go on, with all sorts of unlikely people being brought in, 'good and bad'. We are reminded of the tax collectors and prostitutes entering the kingdom of God in 21:32.

This is not to say that sin doesn't matter. The man at the wedding feast who was dressed inappropriately is not an unfortunate poor man who can't afford nice clothes, but is evidently someone who wants the feast but who can't be bothered to change. This is a warning to intending disciples against thinking that we can have the grace of God without living in the king's way (cf. 7:22–23).

6 Questioning Jesus

It's like a fencing contest, with various groups of people trying to pierce Jesus' defences by their ingenious questions.

You wouldn't expect the Pharisees to be allied with the supporters of Herod, but their question about the sensitive matter of paying taxes to Caesar was designed to trap Jesus: would he speak out against the state (the Herodians were watching), or would he defend the status quo and so upset the people who strongly objected to paying taxes to the Romans on personal, nationalist and theological grounds? Jesus parries their attack first by getting them to show him a coin with the head of Caesar on it, and then with his enigmatic but profound statement about giving Caesar's things to Caesar (he has certain rights) and God's things to God (he is Lord of all).

The Sadducees' sceptical question about the resurrection is no more successful in flooring Jesus. Jesus responds by accusing them of under-estimating the power of God: in the life to come we will be transformed and glorified (to use Paul's word in 1 Corinthians 15), not just carrying on as we always have. Jesus also accuses them of not understanding the true meaning of the Bible: the Sadducees claimed to be followers of Moses, but Jesus argues that the words in the book of Exodus about God being the God of Abraham, Isaac and Jacob point to Abraham, Isaac and Jacob being alive, not just figures of the past. It is a subtle but profound answer, and the people are amazed.

The Pharisees get on no better by asking Jesus about the greatest commandment in the law; indeed, this just leads to his famous and important summary of the law in terms of loving God and loving neighbour.

Finally, Jesus turns the tables and asks them a 50-billion-dollar question about the Messiah. They understood the Messiah to be the son of David, but Jesus quotes Psalm 110 and asks how David (whom they believed to be the author of the psalm) could speak of the Messiah as 'my Lord'. The implied answer is that the Messiah is both son of David and also far greater than David, and the implication is that Jesus is that Messiah to whom God says, 'Sit at my right hand until I put your enemies under your feet.' This is the final thrust in the fencing match, which completely floors his opponents. Jesus is an astonishing teacher, whose words convict but also give life to those who hear them. He is the Lord.

Guidelines

I wonder if we sometimes forget how great Jesus was. He was not just a good teacher who was a bit above average. No, he was astonishing. Whether we look at his dramatic actions (such as riding into Jerusalem on a donkey, overturning the tables in the temple, cursing a fig tree), or at his sharply directed parables, or at his memorable encounters with his intelligent opponents, we see someone who might well have inspired a following.

His authority may be questioned by the temple officials, but it is not in question to us, the readers of the Gospel. He has God's authority: he is God's king entering the holy city, he is lord of the temple, he is the son (far greater than the servants) sent to the vineyard, he is the capstone of the building, and he is the master teacher whose word is a very sharp sword. He is the Lord.

He is also the healer who stops and heals the blind men outside Jericho instead of hurrying on. He heals people in the temple and rejoices at the children's praises. Although so great, he comes as a servant among us, as a slave, and he is going on to give his life as a ransom to bring freedom.

'Hosanna' is a Hebrew word meaning something like 'Save now', but it came to be used as a joyful, enthusiastic greeting. It was an appropriate greeting—even more appropriate than Jesus' disciples understood—and the blind men, after receiving their sight, also responded appropriately, by following Jesus.

Matthew 23:1—25:13

1 Woe to the theologians

What has such a gloomy chapter about the scribes and the Pharisees got to say to us today? The heart of the chapter is seven 'woes' against the professional theologians of the day (the scribes, who were experts in interpreting the Old Testament) and against the most religious group of the time (the Pharisees, who also made much of the Old Testament law).

Historically, the chapter is important because it shows us how Jesus engaged other religious leaders in his day, and how he boldly diagnosed the trouble with their religion. We should not conclude that the Pharisees and others like them were all 'a bad thing'—they weren't; many were very well-intentioned—but religion is often empty, and Jesus has much harsher words to say to the supposedly religious than to the obviously sinful people of the time. The chapter also probably relates to Matthew's context, representing his critique of Jewish religion in synagogue and temple.

The chapter is not just of historical interest, though. Jesus contrasts the ways of the scribes and Pharisees with how it should be among his disciples (for example, in vv. 5–12), and the chapter as a whole has lots to say to the Christian Church, to Christian leaders and to religious people generally.

The principal criticism of the scribes and Pharisees is that they are hypocrites, or play-actors, saying lots of the right things but not practising them, and not helping others to practise. Indeed, the most damning comments of all are the first two woes (vv. 13–15), where the effect of their ministry is described as shutting people out of God's kingdom instead of getting them in, and as making people children of hell rather than children of heaven. This is a very solemn warning to any minister: we are supposed to be saving people, but it is possible to do exactly the opposite in the name of religion—to lead people astray, to damnation, not salvation. If we fail to point people to Jesus and help them into the kingdom, then woe to us indeed.

The other warning in this section is the warning against self-glorification. Religious leadership can so easily be an ego-trip, and religious leaders can get a great kick out of the approval of others. Of course, there is nothing wrong in being on the receiving end of gratitude, and there is no virtue in being unpopular (some clergy seem unfortunately good at upsetting people by their insensitivity or stupidity), but the danger of exalting ourselves rather than Jesus is constant, and it is no accident that Jesus' challenge to his disciples to be humble servants comes once again, in verses 11–12.

2 Religious hypocrisy

Matthew 23:16–39

The word 'woe' is not just an emotional word expressing sorrow or disappointment, but is a warning word that speaks of God's coming judgment (the opposite of the 'happy' word that comes at the start of the so-called beatitudes).

Jesus warns the scribes and Pharisees of their false priorities. They specialized in making fine legal distinctions between this oath and that oath: for example, 'I swear by the gold of the temple' would be a binding oath, 'I swear by the temple' an oath that was not binding. How absurd—but they were learnedly serious about it. They were sticklers for details of the law—for example, about giving tithes of every herb you grew—but were they compassionate to their neighbours? Not to judge from Mark 12:40. Sincerely religious people can miss the point terribly.

Jesus goes on to talk about the outside and the inside: externally, the scribes and Pharisees were shining lights, but inside they were full of greed, self-indulgence, hypocrisy and wickedness—like a nice-looking bowl that inside is full of filth, or like a painted tomb. Tombs were painted white so that they could be seen and not accidentally walked on: they were beautiful outside, but full of bones and other un-cleanness. Earlier in the Gospel we noticed Jesus' stress on inward purity and on the heart (5:8, 28; 15:18–19). How many of us are not guilty of such hypocrisy? There is no room for complacency.

The final 'woe' comments on the discrepancy between the scribes' and Pharisees' claim to honour the prophets and martyrs of previous generations and the way they themselves will treat prophets and godly teachers who are sent to them. Jesus seems here to be anticipating the future persecution of Christian prophets and teachers (something that Matthew may have been quite familiar with, when writing his Gospel). The fact is that these religious leaders are faithful children of their forefathers, completing their murderous work (v. 32). Judgment will no longer be delayed, Jesus says, but will come on this generation. Jesus weeps over the holy city, Jerusalem, because of what is so soon going to happen. False, hypocritical religious leadership is fatal, not trivial. We should pray seriously for those with the heavy responsibility of leadership (James 3:1).

3 The need for endurance

Matthew 24:1–14

The sombre warning about judgment coming on Jerusalem leads us into the last of the major discourses in Matthew's Gospel, in which Jesus talks about the future.

It all starts with the disciples commenting on the temple buildings. The reconstruction of the temple was the brainchild of Herod the Great and began in 19BC; the work was almost complete when Jesus came up for his final visit to Jerusalem, and it was a tremendous sight. The rebuilt temple was huge and magnificent, truly one of the wonders of the world (as Josephus the Jewish historian makes clear). It's not surprising that the disciples comment on it, and nor is it surprising that Jesus' prediction that it would all be destroyed in the foreseeable future made a deep impression (26:60–61).

The disciples probably put two and two together, and assumed that that disastrous event would be the occasion of Jesus' 'parousia'. Parousia means 'coming', and was a word used of a king's visit. They asked Jesus about the likely timing of the two events.

The first part of Jesus' reply is a general description of the whole period leading up to 'the end'. Jesus warns that there will be all sorts of troubles in the world, and that his followers must not be misled into thinking that this means Jesus is about to return; in fact, the wars and other troubles are just 'the beginning of birth pains' (v. 8). Jesus goes on to warn that the Church will be troubled by persecution from outside and by betrayal and false prophecy within. The call to the disciples is therefore to endure. Not that the situation is hopeless: Jesus says that the good news will be preached to all nations, and then the end will come. The sufferings are birth pains, and the kingdom of God that has begun to come with Jesus will finally be established.

Jesus is speaking about the time in which we still live. His warning against being upset by premature speculations about his return, as well as his call to endure when things seem difficult for the Church, remain as relevant as ever in a world where wars, famines, earthquakes and church problems lead some to speculate and others to despair.

4 The future climax

Matthew 24:15–35

Having described the time leading up to 'the end' in general, Jesus becomes specific from verse 15 onwards. He speaks first of an awful event that is going to happen in the Jerusalem temple, and then goes on to describe the coming of the Son of Man on the clouds of heaven.

Jesus uses a phrase found in the book of Daniel to describe the Jerusalem catastrophe. The phrase 'the desolating sacrilege' or 'the abomination of desolation' is usually thought to refer (in Daniel and in the apocryphal book of 1 Maccabees) to the events of 167BC. For certain historical reasons, Antiochus IV, the ruler of the powerful Seleucid empire, attacked Jerusalem in that year. He desecrated the temple, rededicating it to the Greek god Zeus and inaugurating pig sacrifice in that once-holy place. He proceeded to try to abolish the Jewish religion, root and branch. It was an unthinkably awful period for the Jews, but it led to a courageous resistance movement led first by Judas Maccabeus. By 164BC the superpower had been pushed back and the temple was rededicated, an event celebrated ever since by the Jews in the feast of Hanukkah (which means 'Dedication').

Jesus predicts another such event, and speaks of how terrible that time will be, with people continuing to speculate about his imminent return. He warns against such speculation, explaining that his coming, which will follow, will be an unmistakable and universally visible event, like lightning. Jesus speaks of his return as Son of Man on the clouds, and of his angels gathering 'the elect' from the four winds. The reference to the Son of Man on the clouds is reminiscent of Daniel 7:13, where Israel's deliverance from the pagan superpowers of the world (the beasts) is described. Jesus, when he comes, is going to complete God's saving purpose for his people, who are at present scattered to the four winds. So God's kingdom, his rule, will at last be established; the present age will come to an 'end'.

Jesus' teaching here raises all sorts of questions and scholarly opinions. The simplest explanation seems to be that Jesus was anticipating first the destruction of Jerusalem and its temple; this terrible judgment, of which he had spoken in his parables, would come. Indeed, it did come in AD70. But beyond that, Jesus looked forward to his own second coming, when he would complete the work of saving the world that he began in his ministry. We still await that coming. Some people think that Jesus taught that he would return within a generation, but it is preferable to take Jesus' words in verse 34 as referring to the destruction of Jerusalem and to see verse 36 as his agnostic verdict on the time of his return and of the 'end', which would follow the disaster in Jerusalem and the proclaiming of the gospel to the nations (24:14). That proclamation remains the Church's task, until the Lord comes.

5 The thief in the night

Matthew 24:36–44

People love to speculate about the time of the Lord's return, but one of the persistent themes in this discourse about the future is that speculation is futile and should be rejected.

This point is reinforced by the emphatic statement in verse 36 insisting that no one, not even the angels, not even Jesus himself, knows the time. What's the use of speculating in that situation? The point is reinforced also by the explanation that follows, about how 'normal' life will be when Jesus returns, just as it was in the time of

Noah. Business will be going on as usual, and then the Son of Man will return, bringing salvation to some and judgment to others. The picture of one being taken and one left (vv. 40–41) need not be taken as literally as in the popular *Left Behind* books, where the people remaining look around for their colleagues and friends and cannot see them, but the point about the suddenness and seriousness of the Lord's return is clear.

This is why spiritual wakefulness is important. Many English versions translate the Greek of verse 42 as 'keep watch', which could sound as if we are letting excited speculation in the back door again. But the Greek word should be translated 'keep awake', just as you would if you knew that a burglar was going to break into your house at a particular time. The picture of the thief coming could appear to give slightly mixed messages—about the need to keep awake but also about the unpredictability of the Lord's coming—but verse 44 puts the matter succinctly: Christians should be ready for the Lord's return at any time, because his coming will not be expected and cannot be predicted.

The apostle Paul knew much, if not all, of this teaching of Jesus. In 1 Thessalonians 4 and 5 he refers to the Lord returning with a trumpet call, on the clouds, snatching up his people. He also says to the Thessalonians that 'you know very well that the day of the Lord will come like a thief in the night' (5:2). The reason they knew this very well must be because Paul had passed on to them the teaching of Jesus. (It is certain that this teaching does go back to Jesus, since no follower of Jesus would have compared his coming to that of a thief.)

At nearly 2000 years' distance, we may find it much harder to believe that the Lord will return than they did, living just a few years after he had left them. But it makes sense (theologically) that Jesus will return to complete his work, and Paul would urge us to rejoice in the hope that Jesus gives us (Romans 5:2; 15:13). The writer to the Hebrews tells us to encourage one another 'all the more as you see the Day approaching' (Hebrews 10:25).

6 Keep awake

As usual, Jesus uses parables to get his message home. The parable of the thief emphasized the unpredictability of the time. The following parables of the wise and foolish stewards and the wise and foolish virgins make opposite points: the foolish steward did not reckon on how soon his master might return, and the foolish virgins did not reckon on how long it might be till the bridegroom came. The point is clear: Jesus may come soon, or he may come after a long time. 'No one knows the day or the hour' (v. 13).

Let's look briefly at both parables. Wealthy householders would normally employ a household manager (or steward): he would be given almost complete authority in the household in the owner's absence and he would be expected to look after the house and his fellow servants. Jesus pictures a faithful steward who did a good job and was rewarded on his master's return, and a rogue steward who mistreated his fellow servants, getting into drunken ways himself, and who was severely punished when his master returned earlier than he expected. This parable is arguably about leadership in the Church, with a clear challenge to leaders to be responsible in caring for the Church of Christ and other Christians (see Luke 12:41–42; 1 Corinthians 4:1–5), but the parable clearly has wider implications.

As for the parable of the wise and foolish virgins, the picture is of an oriental wedding, starting at an imprecisely fixed hour when the bridegroom and his party arrived. The ten girls waiting with their lamps seem to have had some part to play in the celebrations, but the long delay in the bridegroom's arrival spelled disaster for five of them, who had not prepared for such an eventuality and found themselves too late to get in after they had gone to replenish their lamps. As hearers of the parable, we are not supposed to feel very sorry for the foolish girls— they were foolish—but we are expected to be like the wise girls, being prepared for the long haul.

It has been a long haul, waiting for the Lord's return, with generations coming and going. It is an intriguing possibility that Paul is drawing on this parable when he writes to the Thessalonians about Christians dying before the Lord's return (1 Thessalonians 4:13–18).

Just as the wise virgins fell asleep but then woke up and went into the banquet with the bridegroom, so Paul assures the Thessalonians that Christians who have 'fallen asleep' (that is, died) will wake up when Jesus returns and go to be always with the Lord. We should be encouraged, Paul tells us. We should be encouraged to keep our spiritual lamps burning and not to allow our hope to go out.

Guidelines

There has been quite a sombre tone to much in our reading over the past week, with Jesus warning of terrible judgment to come—on the unbelieving religious leaders, but also on disobedient, unprepared disciples. The thought of weeping and gnashing of teeth is a recurrent theme in Matthew. Judgment is not a popular doctrine these days, and hell in particular has been declared an obsolete idea by some, but it is very unwise for Christians to follow political (or theological) correctness rather than the clear teaching of Jesus. Jesus was more compassionate and loving than any human being before or after him, but he evidently saw no contradiction between that and a belief in God's judgment of wickedness.

There is indeed no contradiction: people who choose, like the wicked steward, to misuse God's gifts, and who abuse God's people, choose judgment for themselves. It would not be good or just for God to say, 'It doesn't matter.' Religious leaders who deceive people and shut them out of the kingdom instead of bringing them in deserve the judgment of God. There is no need to have a lurid medieval picture of hell, but there is no justification for thinking that judgment is unreal or anything but very sad, and weeping and gnashing of teeth expresses that sadness vividly.

As well as pictures of judgment, however, there are pictures too of future salvation—of the Lord gathering his people to be with himself, of the wise virgins going into the wedding celebration, and of the good steward being rewarded, not with a boring part in a heavenly harp orchestra (of course, the harp is a wonderful instrument!), but with greater responsibility in his master's service. The return of Christ is something to be looked forward to. In the early Church, a favourite prayer seems to have been the Aramaic word *Maranatha*, meaning 'Our Lord, come!' (1 Corinthians 16:22).

Matthew 25:14—26:75

1 Serving faithfully

Matthew 25:14–30

It wasn't just pocket money! A talent was worth £100,000 or more, so the master in Jesus' story was entrusting a lot of his wealth to the three servants. His happiness at the good and faithful work of the first two servants is understandable, as is his anger at the servant who just left his talent rotting safely in the ground. The servant is not the timid victim of a hard master, as he made out, but a wicked and lazy servant.

In the English language, the Greek word *talenton* has come to be used for a person's gifts and abilities, and this is rather a good application of the parable. What has God given us? For many of us, it is not big money (for some, it is) but all sorts of other things, including our personalities and our talents. The parable challenges us to use all that God has given us, fruitfully, as servants of Jesus who are looking forward to his return. Jesus' business was the kingdom of God, and he entrusted his business to his disciples, equipping them for that work.

Paul may well have had the parable of the talents at the back of his mind when he wrote about the different gifts that God has given to different members of the Church. Paul compares the different parts of the human body, all of which are important. But some are conspicuously important (ten talents!), others less conspicuously (five or one talent!). 'Do not think of yourself more highly than you ought,' Paul says, but use the gifts you have been given: 'If your gift is prophesying'—a spiritual talent—'then use it in proportion to your faith. If it is serving, then serve; if it is teaching, then teach; if it is encouraging, then encourage; if it is contributing to the needs of others'—a literal talent here!—'then give generously; if it is leadership, then govern diligently; if it is showing mercy'—a sympathetic, caring personality—'then do it cheerfully' (Romans 12:3–8). Peter makes much the same point in 1 Peter 4:10–11: 'Each of you should use

23

whatever gift you have received to serve others, faithfully administering God's grace in its various forms. If you speak, you should do it as those who speak the very words of God. If you serve, you should do it with the strength God provides, so that in all things God may be praised through Jesus Christ.'

Notice how Peter speaks of serving 'faithfully'. In Matthew 25, the master's promise to the good and faithful servant is that he will be rewarded with greater responsibility, and the joyful invitation is, 'Come and share your master's happiness' (vv. 21, 23). Jesus wants to share his happiness with us.

2 Future judgment

Matthew 25:31–46

Jesus ends his teaching about the future with a great picture of the day of judgment. All the nations will be gathered before him (what a claim to authority!) and Jesus, as king, will judge them. Just as a shepherd in Jesus' day would separate the sheep and goats in his flock when night came (though they look similar, goats need more protection at night than sheep), so, Jesus explains, he will separate the righteous and the unrighteous. The righteous will enter 'the kingdom prepared for you since the creation of the world', the kingdom that Jesus announced and began to bring in his ministry; the unrighteous will go to eternal punishment (v. 46).

What makes the difference between the righteous and the unrighteous? The king in the parable explains that the righteous showed him practical kindness—when he was hungry and thirsty, a stranger, lacking clothing, ill or in prison. The unrighteous failed to show him kindness. When quizzed about exactly what he means, he explains that he is thinking of kindnesses done, or not done, 'to one of the least of these brothers of mine' (v. 40).

This famous parable could appear to support the popular view that you get eternal life by being nice to people in need. Even if you are not religious, Jesus identifies with needy people and will let you in if you are kind. That view hardly squares with other teaching of the New Testament, including Matthew's Gospel, where it is clear that the way to life involves believing in Jesus and following him. So what does the parable mean?

Some scholars think that it is about people's response to the disciples—Jesus' spiritual brothers—when they go out on mission. If people welcome the 'little ones' who are Jesus' disciples and support them in need, then they will be rewarded. This view would fit in well with Jesus' words in Matthew 10:40–42.

The alternative view is that Jesus is indeed speaking of kindness shown to needy people in general, but he is not saying that kindness in itself brings salvation. What he is saying is that true, faithful discipleship is not just a matter of saying 'Lord, lord', but of following Jesus and treating other people as he treated them—as his brothers and sisters. Preparing for the Lord's return is not just a matter of exercising talents, but of living in love. As so often, this is the climax of Jesus' teaching about the Christian life.

3 Jesus prepares for his death

Matthew 26:1–16

After looking into the future with Jesus, we now come back into the present with a bump. Verse 2 tells us that Passover and Jesus' arrest are two days away.

Passover (which had effectively been merged with the Feast of Un-leavened Bread) was the greatest festival of the Jewish year, celebrating God's greatest act of salvation. But now, in the crucifixion of the Son of Man, an even greater act of salvation is about to happen.

The route to this salvation is dark. The cautious, strategic plotting of the Jewish authorities is described; the mercenary act of betrayal by Judas is just what they need. But contrasting with these dark schemes is what Jesus calls 'a beautiful deed'. It is beautiful not mainly because of the wonderful perfume that must have filled the house where Jesus was, but because it was a very costly act of love, no doubt of gratitude.

The disciples object, seeing it as an extravagant waste. Were they recalling Jesus' teaching about the dangers of wealth and about the need to give to the poor? Maybe, unless their real motive was to get their hands on the money (cf. John 12:4–6 on Judas' motives, in what may be a different version of the same story). Jesus agrees on the importance of giving to the poor, of course, but he interprets the woman's action entirely positively, seeing it as wholly appropriate to the moment, and explaining it as 'preparing me for burial'. Anointing the body was a normal burial procedure.

Jesus was about to undergo the loneliest, hardest time he would ever face, being betrayed and abandoned by his friends. The woman's devotion was an encouragement to him, and indeed was seen by Jesus as the proper response to the Gospel events that were unfolding, though she cannot have seen that significance herself.

'Do you love me?' was the question Jesus would later put to Peter (John 21:15–17). It is the question we need to ask in the face of what Jesus did for us in his passion and crucifixion.

4 The final meal

Matthew 26:17–30

Jesus knew well what was going to happen: his *kairos* ('appointed time') was near. His first step was to celebrate Passover with his disciples, and he seems already to have made arrangements with the man in whose house they were going to eat the Passover meal. Was this man a contact from a previous visit to Jerusalem? John's Gospel tells us that Jesus made several visits to Jerusalem during his ministry.

Passover would usually be a joyful celebratory meal, but Jesus' devastating prediction that one of the disciples was going to betray him was extremely and understandably upsetting. As they tried to work out who he could mean, Jesus commented that it was all part of God's plan, though still a terrible thing for the person concerned.

The disciples had consistently found Jesus' teaching about his coming death incomprehensible. It just did not fit their idea of messiahship, nor their own ambitions; they had given up so much to follow Jesus.

It is in that context that Jesus' actions with the bread and the wine make sense. Jesus was into parables and acted parables (for example, riding into Jerusalem on a donkey and turning over the tables in the temple). Now, using bread and wine, he shows his followers that his coming death is a Passover sacrifice bringing them salvation and the forgiveness of sins. Jesus does not just give an explanation of the theology of his coming death, but by getting them to eat 'my body' and drink 'my blood' he communicates the truth about his coming death in a powerful and profound way. He is giving his life for them, the friends whom he has chosen and loved.

It was a lesson they would not forget, and indeed that was the point. Jesus intended the acted parable to be one through which they would remember him, until the coming of his kingdom when he and his disciples would feast again. It was not magic, but it was and is a powerful communication of the amazing love that took Jesus to the cross, and it has inspired and continues to inspire Christians as they look forward to Jesus' return.

5 The final choice

Matthew 26:31–56

As we leave the upper room and come to Gethsemane, it is as though the darkness closes in. Jesus tells the disciples that they will fall away. They are indignant, especially Peter, but before long they have all fled. Judas leads an arresting party who take Jesus into custody, and Peter will soon deny Jesus.

In the garden itself, Jesus' closest friends, whom he asks to stay awake and to pray with him, all fall asleep. So it is without human support that Jesus goes through spiritual torture; he faces temptation such as he has never experienced before. The temptation is to opt out of the will of God, to run away. Jesus indeed prays for the awful cup to be taken from him, but adds, 'Yet not as I will, but as you will' (v. 39). Jesus battles in prayer, three times, and wins through. So at the end, instead of running away, he says, 'Rise, let us go! Here comes my betrayer!' (v. 46).

Gethsemane was a key moment for Jesus, and gives us a glimpse of the cost of the cross. Hebrews 5:7 says, 'He offered prayers and petitions with loud cries and tears to the one who could save him from death, and he was heard because of his reverent submission.' He was heard, but he was not saved from death; instead, through death he 'became the source of eternal salvation' (Hebrews 5:9).

Gethsemane shows us Jesus, but also challenges us to pray. Jesus prayed and prayed and prayed, and went on to save the world. Peter slept three times, and went on to deny Jesus. If Jesus needed to pray, how much more do we, so that we 'will not fall into temptation. The spirit is willing, but the body is weak' (v. 41). In a real sense, Jesus won the battle of the cross in prayer in Gethsemane; we need to beware of going boldly into God's service, like Peter, without the preparation of prayer. Jesus' memorable statement about people who draw the sword dying by the sword (v. 52) is a warning against trusting in human power rather than trusting in God and looking for his victory.

6 Condemnation

Matthew 26:57–75

They had got Jesus, but they struggled to legitimate their murderous plans for him. They needed to do so, since the Sanhedrin was a legal court, indeed the supreme Jewish court (under the Romans); so they tried to find charges against Jesus. But it was not easy to find any charges that could remotely be made to stick.

Jesus' critical attitude to the temple was their first promising line, but they could not get Jesus to confirm that he had spoken about destroying and rebuilding the temple in three days. The accusation was almost true, but not quite: Jesus had spoken of the temple being destroyed, of himself as greater than the temple, and of his death and resurrection in three days.

Jesus did not attempt to explain this to the Sanhedrin, however; he was silent until he was asked if he was 'the Christ, the Son of God'. His answer then was (literally), 'You said' (v. 64). This is probably to be understood as a 'yes' from Jesus. In any case, Jesus goes on to speak of himself as 'the Son of Man' and to tell the authorities that one day they will see him sitting on God's right hand and coming on the clouds of heaven. There are clear echoes here of Daniel 7:13. For the authorities, it was all that they wanted: Jesus was clearly making an outrageous claim about his relationship to God. He was a blasphemer who deserved death.

While the court struggled to condemn Jesus, Peter struggled to be faithful to Jesus. In fact, he hardly seems to have struggled at all, but to have denied Jesus at the first opportunity, when challenged by a servant girl (not a tough soldier, but a servant girl, and then by another girl). And he didn't just deny Jesus a little, but emphatically, cursing and swearing. It is no wonder that when the cock crowed he broke down. The flesh was weak. Peter had been cocky and not prayerful.

Guidelines

The Lord's supper is sometimes called the eucharist (from the Greek word for 'thanksgiving'), sometimes the mass, sometimes holy communion. Communion means 'sharing', and the last supper was indeed a very special or holy sharing. Jesus shared the bread and the wine to help his disciples understand and remember that in his coming death he was dying for them and sharing himself with them; in receiving the bread and wine they were sharing in his death and life.

However, far from being a sharing and unifying meal (as it should be, see 1 Corinthians 10:17), the holy communion has often been very divisive in the Church, with different ideas about its exact meaning.

I find two things helpful—first, to think of it as an acted parable, so much more powerful than simple words, because we see and taste and take it to ourselves. Second, I find the comparison of a kiss helpful. What is a kiss? Answer: the meeting of two pairs of lips and the exchange of molecules of air and germs. Is that true? Yes, on one level. Yet, in the context of a loving relationship, a kiss is far, far more. It is the expression of love; even more than that, a kiss conveys love from one person to another. Bread and wine are physical, molecular substances, but in the context of the Lord's supper they convey the loving death of Jesus to the hearts and minds of those who are in relationship with him. It is not a perfect analogy, and it leaves questions unanswered, but it is an understanding that helps me, as I remember the Lord and his death and receive the signs of bread and wine.

Matthew 27—28

1 All are guilty

Matthew 27:1–26

I expect that if we met them at a party we would find that they were all normal, interesting, even pleasant people—yes, even Judas, Pilate, the Jewish leaders and the members of the crowd. Yet they were all guilty of the blood of Jesus.

Judas realized his guilt and committed suicide. There is a different, rather gory account of his death in Acts 1:18–19, which suggests that Judas himself bought the field, whereas our account suggests that it was the Jewish authorities, using Judas' money (v. 7). The accounts agree, however, about the 'field of blood' being associated with Judas' betrayal of Jesus.

Pilate recognized the innocence of Jesus, even before his wife's nightmare. He tried to pass the buck, first by offering the crowd a choice between Jesus and Barabbas. When that failed to win Jesus' release, he publicly washed his hands before the crowd, as though that excused him of his responsibility. He claimed, 'I am innocent of this man's blood' (v. 24), but of course he wasn't. He gave the order for the release of guilty Barabbas, for the scourging of Jesus and for the crucifixion.

The crowd, egged on by the religious authorities, did not claim innocence; on the contrary, they uttered those chilling words, 'His blood be on us and on our children' (v. 25). Those words have been used, tragically, by Christians (so-called) to justify the persecution of Jews, and Matthew has been accused of anti-Semitism in including these words in the Gospel.

It is true that Matthew does see the Jews, in particular the Jewish authorities, as especially guilty. They are religious people (hence their scruples about the use of Judas' 'blood money'), yet their hatred of Jesus is unqualified. But although Matthew highlights their guilt, with good historical reason, the fact is that everyone is guilty for the shedding of Jesus' innocent blood—Judas the idealist, Pilate the politician in a difficult position, the religious authorities, the crowds, even the disciples who failed Jesus, and certainly later disciples of Jesus who have taken up the sword against the Jews and other religious groups. And that is the point: Jesus is the silent lamb who is slaughtered, because 'we all, like sheep, have gone astray… and the Lord has laid on him the iniquity of us all' (Isaiah 53:6).

2 Truthful mockery

Matthew 27:27—44

Judas and Pilate may have had qualms but, once the sentence had been pronounced and Jesus handed over to the soldiers, there was no kindness shown to the prisoner (or almost none: see v. 34). There was no Geneva convention about treating prisoners well and not humiliating them; on the contrary, crucifixion was all to do with humiliating prisoners.

The soldiers played a mocking game with Jesus before taking him to the unpleasant practical business of crucifixion. Those crucified with Jesus also insulted him, and the religious leaders mocked him as well. Each group thought they were joking in what they said, but there was massive truth in each cruel joke.

The soldiers joked about Jesus as 'king of the Jews' (that being the official charge against him); but we as readers of Matthew's Gospel know that Jesus was indeed king of the Jews. The two crucified with Jesus (Matthew doesn't tell us about the repentant thief) mocked the idea of Jesus destroying and rebuilding the temple, and challenged Jesus to save himself and to come down from the cross, 'if you are the Son of God' (v. 40). We, as readers of the Gospel, know that Jesus was Son of God, who could have saved himself but who was dying as the final sacrifice to bring a new temple and new life for the world. The religious leaders commented on how Jesus saved others and on his trust in God, and challenged him now to save himself and prove himself the Son of God. They were mostly right in what they said, except that Jesus was saving others by not saving himself; he was showing himself the Son of God by trusting in God to the end. He was drinking the cup.

The one person who doesn't mock is Simon of Cyrene (v. 32). He is in Jerusalem on pilgrimage, passing by, and he finds himself press-ganged into helping out with this horrible business. It could have ruined his Passover, but there is some reason to think that it brought him to faith in Jesus, the one who saved and was saving others (see the reference to his sons in Mark 15:21—evidently they were members of the Church; see also Romans 16:13).

3 It is finished

Matthew 27:45–56

It was midday, but there was extraordinary darkness, both physical darkness and also spiritual darkness, as Jesus experienced God-forsakenness, crying out.

In the story, other people have said a lot of mainly foolish things; Jesus has said very little, but the cry of desolation in verse 46 (the words taken from Psalm 22) indicate the suffering that Jesus experienced: for the Son of God to experience the cup of divine judgment was hell.

The misunderstanding and fussing of the bystanders missed the point entirely. Then Jesus cried out again. It is John's Gospel that records Jesus as crying, 'It is finished', but the other Gospels, including Matthew, agree that Jesus' death brought to an end and to completion his work of saving us from our sins.

The tearing of the huge curtain that separated the inner sanctuary of the temple, the holy of holies, from the public areas of the temple was, in scientific terms, the result of the earthquake—presumably. Seen theologically, it represents the opening up of God's presence so that we may go in, through the death of Jesus (Hebrews 10:19–20). The earthquake also burst open tombs in the Jerusalem area, and after Jesus' resurrection various people had visions of Old Testament saints. Only Matthew tells us this curious story, but its significance is clear: Jesus' death is the defeat of death, and his resurrection is the beginning of the resurrection of the dead. The Jews believed that the resurrection of the dead would happen 'at the end of the age', but Matthew tells us that it began, in history, with Jesus.

The reaction of the soldiers, appropriately, was of fear, but also of recognition that 'Surely he was the Son of God' (v. 54). Onlookers had joked about Jesus as God's Son, but it was no joking matter; it was and is the most serious and wonderful and joyful truth about the one who died on the cross.

4 The final service

Matthew 27:55–66

Religion is sometimes seen as a women's thing, or for women and children and not really for men. Jesus, however, inspired men just as much as women. Some of Jesus' followers were thoroughly masculine men, but when it came to Jesus' arrest, even the weather-hardened fishermen Peter, Andrew, James and John ran away. It was some of the Galilean women who had followed and given practical support to Jesus during his ministry who stayed with him as he died. They were probably less at risk from the authorities than the male disciples, but even they were wise to watch from a distance.

One man who showed courage was Joseph from Arimathea. Luke tells us that he was a member of the Jewish Sanhedrin, and says that he did not agree to the death of Jesus (Luke 23:50–51). Now he asked Pilate for the body of Jesus. The Jewish burial practice involved placing the corpse in a cave (natural or artificial), where it would decompose; then, many months later, the bones would be gathered and put in a stone box (an ossuary) for final burial. Joseph put Jesus in a new tomb that he had cut for himself, rolling a large stone before the door. It was probably near the crucifixion site, where the Church of the Holy Sepulchre in Jerusalem is today. The church is now inside the city, but archaeologists have shown that originally the hill beneath the church was outside the walls of the city, near a road leading into the city, and that it has burial caves adjacent to it.

Only Matthew describes the setting of a guard over the tomb. It was a perfectly logical move, given the authorities' determination to suppress the Christian movement and given Jesus' prediction, before his death, that he would rise again (a prediction found in all the Gospels). It was logical and intelligent, but futile (Acts 2:24).

5 God had triumphed

It was a shattering event in more senses than one. Experiencing an earthquake was bad enough, but if you were also guarding a tomb for the Roman governor and it was broken into while under your custody, then that was a disaster (and might well cost you your life). If, in addition to that, you saw a dazzling angel, you would surely shake and become 'like dead men' (v. 4).

The women followers of Jesus were also afraid, but their fear was turned to joy and to worship, as first the angel and then the risen Jesus himself said to them, 'Do not be afraid' (vv. 5, 10). The angels showed them the evidence of the empty tomb; Jesus showed them himself. Both the angels and Jesus told them to instruct the disciples to return to Galilee, where they would see him for themselves.

Quite what the guards really thought had happened, we will never know; they didn't see the risen Jesus. Matthew tells us that they were bribed to say that the disciples had stolen the body. It was not a very good story, and could itself get them into trouble, but they needed some explanation, and they were promised that they would be all right if they did as they were told. So this became the official 'alternative' explanation to the Christian claim that Jesus had risen from the dead.

For Matthew, this is the final denial of the truth on the part of the religious authorities. They would not accept Jesus, even now, and their self-preserving deceit would mislead generations of Jews and others too, and help prevent them from finding the forgiveness of sins that the Saviour came to bring.

Matthew wants people to see the risen Jesus, to believe in him and to worship him, as the women did.

6 Jesus' authority

What a climax—a mountain-top experience, indeed! It sums up so much of what Matthew has been telling us. First, there is Jesus, risen from the dead, worthy of worship, with all authority in heaven and earth. The wording is reminiscent of Daniel 7:14, which describes the one like a Son of Man, to whom dominion is given.

Jesus' authority is clear from the mandate given to the disciples to baptize people in the name of the Father, the Son and the Holy Spirit (v. 19). Jesus is not just a man, but part of the divine Trinity (which is the way the Church will come to describe God in his majesty).

Jesus' authority is clear too in the command that they should teach people to obey 'everything that I have commanded you' (v. 20). It is not the law given by Moses that is now the decisive word, but Jesus' astonishing and wonderful teaching that Matthew has set before us in the Gospel.

Jesus' authority is clear too from the final promise that 'I am with you always' (v. 20). Jesus is Immanuel, God with us, not just during his ministry but to the very end of time.

His authority calls for worship (even if some doubt, finding the good news almost unbelievable), for mission (so that others, not just Jews now but people from all nations, will come into his flock and family), for passing on his teaching (so that people know how to live), and for trust in his presence and protection.

The story of Jesus thus reaches a glorious climax in Matthew, and we appropriately stop to worship at Jesus' feet. But we are not to stop there. The story is one that we are to take to others, so that God's saving work will reach all the nations of the world, and then the end will come.

Guidelines

The resurrection stories differ in the four Gospels, and some people say that they are contradictory. They are also suspicious of certain elements, such as Matthew's story about the guard being bribed; this is not found in any of the other Gospels and sounds like polemic against the Jews. So maybe we are inclined to doubt, like some of the disciples (and like Thomas in John 20:24–31).

Matthew knows that there are doubts around. In his context, the main unbelieving explanation of the resurrection is the story that the disciples stole the body. Matthew wants to lay that doubt to rest with his account of where that unlikely story came from. The suggestion that the disciples stole the body and invented the idea of the resurrection is quite incredible, and other doubts about the resurrection have little more foundation. Yes, there are differences between the Gospels, but Luke assures us that the risen Jesus appeared many times to his disciples, and so we would expect different stories (Acts 1:3); and even when it is the same basic story, independent witnesses will normally tell things differently.

For Matthew, as for the other Gospel writers, the evidence for the resurrection is (a) the empty tomb; and (b) the appearances of Jesus. The fact that the Gospel writers all agree that the empty tomb was found by women is remarkable, given the suspicion of women's testimony in the ancient world. As well as the Gospels, Paul's references to the resurrection and the appearances of the risen Christ in 1 Corinthians 15 are of great importance, since we can date that letter to around AD55 and its testimony much earlier ('I passed on to you... what I also received').

Jesus' resurrection has been called 'the best-attested fact in history'. Matthew would want us to see it also, along with the rest of the story of Jesus, as the best fact in history. What makes it such a good fact is its continuing relevance to Matthew's readers and to us: Jesus has all authority, his teaching is the way to life and the way to live, he is with us always, and we have very good news for the world.

ABRAHAM

Abraham is one of the momentous figures of world history. His significance can be summed up in two of the things that the Bible says about him. He is the 'friend of God' (Isaiah 41:8), and he is the 'ancestor of a multitude of nations' (Genesis 17:4). These come together in the fact that the world's two largest faiths, Christianity and Islam, together with the faith out of which they grew, Judaism, are often called 'the Abrahamic religions', for Abraham is the foundational figure common to all three. Abraham is a man from the mists of antiquity whose depth of engagement with God has continued to be fruitful in an astonishing variety of ways.

What kind of stories are the stories featuring Abraham? It is important not to prejudge what we think the material ought to be, rather than trying to discern what it actually is. First, it is clear that the material was written many centuries later than the events it depicts. Even on the traditional assumption that Moses wrote the material, he would have been writing some 400 years later. Scholars have shown that, in all likelihood, the material was initially passed on orally and later written by several different hands, all subsequent to Moses.

Second, the stories seem to presuppose aspects of Israel's own history with God, which are compressed into single episodes of great depth and resonance. There are perhaps similarities to the way in which the stories of Robin Hood compress the history and ideals of several centuries of English experience into a fixed cast of characters and a single historical context. Thus, the portrayal of Abraham is inseparable from the continuing impact that he continued to have within ancient Israel.

We need, therefore, to take the stories with total imaginative seriousness, just as we do any worthwhile story. At the same time, we must recognize that the reality underlying the text is complex, so taking the text seriously does not mean supposing that the storyline could be at all straightforwardly transposed into a historian's account of the early second millennium BC.

Quotations are taken from the New Revised Standard Version of the Bible.

1 God's call and promise

Genesis 12:1–3

These words are the keynote for the whole story that follows. For Abram (whose name is changed to Abraham later on: Genesis 17:5), engagement with God means not unusual mental states, glorified tribal loyalties or tenuous speculations. It is a matter of call and promise from God, envisaging trust and obedience from the human recipient.

God's opening words (v. 1) are a summons to 'go', to leave what is familiar and safe, the places Abram knows and the people he knows and who know him. Where he is to go, he does not know in advance, but will only discover as he goes; understanding will come with obedience.

Abram may naturally be fearful about going. To leave one's familiar context may be a journey into extinction and oblivion. So God reassures him with a promise that reveals the purpose of the divine summons. God will give the married but childless Abram (Genesis 11:29–30) so many descendants that he, through his descendants, will become a famous nation (v. 2). Moreover, God will so commit himself to Abram that those favourable or hostile towards Abram will encounter God's favour or hostility accordingly (v. 3a). This will be so marked that Abram will in some sense become a worldwide blessing (though obviously 'the earth' has a wider meaning for today's reader than for the ancient writer).

The sense in which Abram will become a blessing can be taken in more than one way. The NRSV footnote, 'by you all the families of the earth shall bless themselves', envisages Abram becoming a model to be emulated, such that when people want to invoke a picture of a blessed existence they will invoke Abram (in the form of his descendants, Israel) and say, 'May God make you like Abram/Israel' (rather as the leader of a poor nation might say, 'May we become rich like America'). This is the idiom of blessing found in Genesis 48:20. In this sense, Abram is reassured that his obedience to God will lead to his being recognized as a model of what life should be like.

The words 'in you all the families of the earth shall be blessed' suggest that Abram is to be a vehicle of God's blessing to the world.

What God promises is not only for Abram's reassurance and benefit, but for the well-being of others also. This is the basic sense that Paul finds in the text (Galatians 3:6–9).

2 An early exodus

Genesis 12:4—13:2

In obedience to God, Abram sets out, taking his family with him. He travels through Canaan, in the middle of which, at Shechem, God tells him that this is the land of the promise. But Abram continues to journey southwards (we are not sure why), with the result that, in time of famine, he keeps on journeying out of the promised land altogether, into Egypt.

Abram's time in Egypt looks odd. Should we find fault with him for lying and being faithless, or should we enjoy the sight of a wily Abram outsmarting dumb Egyptians? On any reckoning, Abram's behaviour seems ambiguous and hard to evaluate, though it is difficult not to find fault with him to some extent against the wider backdrop of scripture.

Whatever we make of Abram, however, the significance of the story may lie on a different level, for what happens here encapsulates what happens later to Israel at the end of Genesis and the beginning of Exodus. In time of famine, the people of Israel go down to Egypt and initially prosper there. When they are oppressed, the Lord afflicts Pharaoh with plagues, and Pharaoh sends them away. The Israelites leave with considerable herds, silver and gold. Abram's story encapsulates that of Israel.

This is particularly important for understanding how to read these Genesis narratives. The processes by which the stories were formed have drawn deep analogies between Abram and the nation of Israel, presumably to enable Israel to find itself, as it were, in these stories, which tell of a time before Israel as such existed. This is similar to the classic means by which Christians have tended to read the Old Testament down the ages—that is, as figuration or typology, seeing patterns in the text that resonate with patterns in the Christian life. The stories are *our* stories, which is not to say that they are not also the stories of Jews, but that we should be looking for ways of finding ourselves within the dynamics of the text.

Finally, we see that Abram has, in effect, left the two great centres of early civilization—Mesopotamia, where Ur and Haran were located (11:31), and Egypt. This is a tacit testimony to Israel's vocation and, by extension, that of the Church, not to assimilate to contemporary culture but to be a distinctive people, set apart by obedience to God's call.

3 A costly choice

Genesis 13:2–18

Abram returns to the land of Canaan and, as he had looked to God previously, so he looks to God now (vv. 2–4). However, typical problems of life soon arise. The very wealth that Abram enjoys, and which is shared by his nephew Lot, gives rise to conflict (vv. 5–7). There is not enough room for them both (which initially sounds surprising, but is explained by the note in verse 7b that the land had plenty of other inhabitants as well).

What is Abram to do? As the head of the family, he could resolve the problem by imposing a solution upon Lot and his herders: he could take Lot's herders as his own, or he could send them away to find somewhere else to live. Abram opts for a form of the latter solution, but in a way that speaks volumes within the wider context of scripture: power is truly realized not in imposing upon but in enabling others. Abram offers Lot the choice of where to settle, thus taking the risk that he himself will be left with second-best (vv. 8–9).

Lot looks around and, indeed, chooses what looks to be the best territory. The Jordan valley is described in glowing terms. It has the kind of water supply and fertility that would mark the very garden of God (like Eden), or Egypt, where the Nile irrigates the land. It must be the best place to live, so Lot goes there (vv. 10–13).

Yet the story is strongly ironic, for the best and most fertile place is going to become the most blasted and arid (v. 10b). The reason for this is a factor that Lot apparently failed to consider significant in his deciding where to settle—the wickedness and corruption of the inhabitants (v. 13). The story is parabolic of the foolishness of making decisions based on superficial attractiveness.

Only after Lot has gone, when Abram has had to face the possible costliness of his generosity, does God speak again to Abram. As though matching Abram's generosity, God's initial, rather brief, promise (12:7) is expanded in glowing terms (vv. 14–16), and Abram is invited to savour his inheritance by walking through it in a way that will symbolically celebrate God's gift (v. 17).

Abram then settles at Hebron, where he builds another altar, which seems to symbolize a dedication of the place to God. Abram is not complacent about what God is giving him.

4 Strange encounters

Genesis 14:1–24

The account of the military campaign that fills the first two-thirds of this chapter is unusual within the Abraham stories, not least for its numerous names of people and places, but the basic storyline is clear.

The kings in the Jordan valley rebel against their overlord, Chedorlaomer. Chedorlaomer comes and defeats the rebels and, for good measure, plunders them; Lot (who is presumably already discovering that living in the Jordan valley is not all that it looked to be) is taken off as part of the plunder. Abram has enough resources to pursue and defeat Chedorlaomer's troops in a night attack and to rescue Lot and retrieve the rest of the plunder as well (vv. 1–16).

This sets the scene for two encounters that are the real interest of the narrative. Abram meets both the king of Sodom and the king of Salem (that is, Jerusalem: cf. Psalm 76:2. 'The King's Valley' is probably close to Jerusalem: cf. 2 Samuel 18:18). One represents a place of evil and corruption, the other a place of God's holy presence. How will Abram interact with each?

The king of Sodom comes to meet the victorious Abram to negotiate terms for the return of what was plundered from Sodom (v. 17). Surprisingly, however, before the king of Sodom can say a word, Melchizedek king of Salem appears with bread and wine, presumably as a gift to refresh Abram (v. 18a), though his gift has naturally acquired rich resonances in Christian imagination. Melchizedek is not only king but also a priest, and he blesses Abram, pronouncing that the deity who made heaven and earth is also the one who has enabled Abram to be victorious over his numerically superior enemies (vv. 18b–20a). Abram says nothing, but enacts a response of grateful recognition by giving a tithe of his spoil to this mysterious priest-king (v. 20b).

The king of Sodom now makes his negotiating proposal, one that sounds fairly generous (v. 21). But Abram declines. He has sworn to the deity by whom he has just been blessed—and 'God most High' is none other than the God Israel recognizes, the Lord (v. 22a)—that he will not be in any way beholden to the king of Sodom as he is to the other king (of Jerusalem). All he will keep is for those who have helped him (vv. 22–24). For himself, a sufficient reward for his campaign is that he has received God's blessing.

5 The meaning of faith

Genesis 15:1–21

Did Abram have second thoughts after declining enrichment from his military campaign? At any rate, God speaks to reassure Abram and promises him rich reward (v. 1), in a way that resonates with Jesus' promise to his disciples who followed him at great cost (Mark 10:28–30).

For the first time in the story, Abram's words to God are recorded. Remarkably, Abram does not thank God for the promise just made, but rather queries it: how can God's assurance be meaningful when God's prime promise of descendants remains unfulfilled in any satisfying way (vv. 2–3)? God does not brush aside Abram's words as in any way improper, but rather meets them with two specific assurances. First, it will indeed be Abram's own offspring, not a slave (or even Lot) who will be his heir (v. 4). Second, Abram's descendants will be like the stars on a clear night, wondrously beyond counting (v. 5).

Abram still 'only' has God's word for this. On one level, nothing has changed, yet Abram is willing to take God at his word and trust him (v. 6a), a response of which God clearly approves (v. 6b). So basic is such trust to any real relationship with God that Paul looked to this passage as spelling out the heart of that which also characterizes Christian faith (Romans 4; Galatians 3).

God's approval takes shape in a further promise, to give to Abram the land in which he is living as a resident alien (v. 7). Again, Abram (the model of trust) responds with a query (v. 8). Again God takes it seriously, thereby showing that a genuine and trusting relationship with God has space within it for question and answer.

God's answer is a strange one. Abram is told to perform a ritual that has no parallel elsewhere in the Old Testament. He is not to sacrifice the animals, but to slaughter them, divide them (except the birds), and wait (vv. 9–11). As the darkness of night comes on, an even deeper, fearful darkness comes upon Abram in himself. Within this darkness God speaks strange words whose main tenor is 'wait': the fulfilment of God's promises will not be for a long time, and Abram himself will die before he sees it (vv. 12–16).

Then, however, God guarantees the promise that the land will belong to Abram's descendants. The fire represents God's presence, as at the burning bush, and passing between the divided animals symbolizes God's self-commitment to his promise to Abram (vv. 17–21).

6 An aborted exodus

Genesis 16:1–16

Waiting is hard. Despite the renewal of God's promise to Abram that he will have offspring, nothing happens, so Sarai impatiently tries to exploit a possible loophole. God had said that the offspring would be Abraham's own, and would be numerous, but he had not specified that she, Sarai, had to be the mother. Since her continuing inability to conceive seems to be by the hand of God, then perhaps a substitute would serve the purpose (vv. 1–3).

But the bright idea instantly runs aground on the rocks of raw human emotions—contempt, jealousy, resentment. Sarai turns on the crowing Hagar and maltreats her so badly, with Abram's weak acquiescence, that Hagar runs away to the wilderness (vv. 4–6).

Here we have a remarkable kind of exodus in reverse. A Hebrew oppresses an Egyptian, who flees to the wilderness, where God is encountered (vv. 7–8). The angel of the Lord has three things to say to Hagar—bad news, then good news.

The bad news is that this time there is to be no escape from oppression. Hagar must return to the place and person she hates, and submit (v. 9). It is a hard word, but a reminder that the will of God may include enduring hardship as well as being delivered from it.

However, the angel renews to Hagar the promise of countless offspring in terms similar to those earlier used with Abram (v. 10). She, through her children, will flourish just like Abram. Maybe, she might suppose, she is to be the channel of God's promise to Abram after all.

So, thirdly, the angel makes clear that Hagar's son has a destiny distinct from Abram's. His name is to be a permanent reminder of God's concern for Hagar in her suffering (v. 11), but he is not to be the blessing to others. Rather, he and his descendants will be wild and not peaceable, and that will be the reason for their being set apart (v. 12). In this regard, Ishmael is like Cain (cf. Genesis 4:15). It is striking that these 'awkward' people are no less the object of God's concern and promises than the chosen line of Abram. As Job also has to learn, God's purposes are wider and less comfortable than what we might naturally imagine.

Hagar is awed by her encounter, and commemorates it in the name of the place (vv. 13–14). Without more ado, she returns to her unwelcome home to fulfil God's purposes there for the time being (vv. 15–16).

Guidelines

The great Danish thinker Søren Kierkegaard once said of the Church Father John Chrysostom that 'he gesticulated with his whole existence' —that is to say, who he was pointed to God. That is surely also true of Abraham, whose whole being, whatever his ups and downs, speaks of the realities of life with God. May it be true also of us, that we 'gesticulate with our existence'.

1 A promise and a symbol

Genesis 17:1–27

Years pass. The waiting continues, but its end is near. God appears again to Abram and renews his promise, specifying that this promise is a covenant, which will mean mutual obligation (vv. 1–2). God has three distinct things to say.

First, the covenant is God's promise. As before, descendants and land are promised, with a fuller specification now than previously. On the one hand, the countless descendants will in fact be not one nation but many, and this is so significant that Abram's name is to be changed to Abraham as a permanent reminder (in a Hebrew wordplay). On the other hand, the land is granted in perpetuity (vv. 3–8).

Second, Abraham's role in the covenant is spelled out. Abraham's present and future family is to have every male circumcised, a requirement that includes slaves who are not blood members of the household so that there is no distinction within the household (vv. 9–14).

Why circumcision? It was a widespread ancient practice and, indeed, there is an assumption within the text that it is familiar to Abraham already. Its symbolic meaning is not spelled out, and so must be inferred. Since the wider concern in the story is God's promise of descendants, circumcision marks the human involvement in producing descendants. In the very act of sexual intercourse there is a reminder that the children who may be born as a result are to be understood not only in familiar human categories (love, family continuity) but also in terms of a fulfilment of God's promise. Moreover, the fact that babies only eight days old are to be circumcised, when frequently in other cultures circumcision was a rite of puberty, means that circumcision also comes to symbolize the dedication of newborn life to God.

Third, God tells Abraham that it is his wife Sarai, and no one else, who is to be the mother of Abraham's descendants; and her name is changed also, as a memorial to this (vv. 15–16).

After all the waiting, and the increasing age of Sarah and himself, Abraham's initial response is incredulity. Surely God's promise must be realized through his existing son, Ishmael (vv. 17–18). But God means what he says, though this does not exclude Ishmael from blessing also, and to underline it, for the first time a date is given for Sarah's bearing a son (vv. 19–22).

Abraham then responds as a model of obedience to God's commandment (vv. 23–27).

2 Negotiating with God

The Lord appears to Abraham, remarkably taking the form of three men (a mysterious detail most memorably captured in Christian imagination by Rublev's icon of the Trinity). Abraham and Sarah offer hospitality to those who initially appear simply to be travellers (vv. 1–8), thereby modelling practical care for others (cf. Hebrews 13:1–3).

God's message parallels that at the end of chapter 17. This time the emphasis is on Sarah's incredulity. Even though Sarah's laughter is kept to herself, the Lord knows about it and overrides it. He reaffirms God's power to transform what seems humanly impossible. Sarah is cowed by this, and God's mild rebuke is perhaps intended also as a reminder of the divine power that reaches what is usually inaccessible (vv. 9–15).

Abraham's hospitable escort of his visitors as they set off for Sodom might be the end of the story (v. 16), but in fact issues are intensified. In a remarkable divine soliloquy, some of the implications of Abraham's being chosen to be the father of many and a blessing to all are spelled out. Abraham's call involves access to God's purposes, which are to be understood in terms of justice and righteousness; God wants patterns of human living that display something of his own integrity (vv. 17–19). In the light of this, God engages Abraham with regard to his moral concerns in this context—Sodom and Gomorrah (Lot's home), where human life is reputed to be corrupt, the opposite of what God looks for (vv. 20–21).

Of the three men, apparently two go off while one remains to speak with Abraham, to give Abraham opportunity to display and develop qualities appropriate to his role as chosen by God. Abraham has to explore something of what justice really means (vv. 23–33). Although he appears to speak confidently (v. 25), this is a dialogue where Abraham also feels himself to be on a knife edge, probing uncertainly (vv. 27, 30, 32). This is not like haggling in the bazaar, for the Lord sets no opening price. Abraham himself sets all the terms, and the Lord always acquiesces. One issue is that the upright and the corrupt should not receive identical treatment, for right and wrong must matter (v. 25). The other is that a few upright may have a leavening effect so that the corrupt receive mercy (v. 24). Both issues are probed, but neither is resolved; learning God's values is a continuing process.

3 Judgment and mercy

Genesis 19:1–29

The story of the two men/angels in Sodom begins straightforwardly, with Lot offering hospitality similar to that of Abraham (vv. 1–3). Yet it rapidly turns nasty, with an aggressive visit by the locals (vv. 4–5). Lot's attempt to defend his guests does nothing for the modern reader and within the text is rudely rejected: what right have incomers to try to tell the locals what to do? (vv. 6–9). As brutality is about to take over, Lot's visitors intervene and gain breathing space by turning their attackers' vision in upon themselves (vv. 10–11).

The nature of the Sodomites' sin has traditionally been construed as 'homosexuality' but more recently by some as abuse of hospitality. Such categories in such an antithesis are unhelpful, for the intended offence is clearly same-sex rape and the visit is an attack on strangers; the picture is one of aggression that takes the form of unbridled sexual appetite and violence.

The men make clear that the purpose of their presence is to enact God's judgment upon the sin of Sodom; but, presumably because of Abraham's interaction with God, Lot and his family are not to be swept away with the corrupt, and so Lot is given an opportunity to rescue his family. Those locals who are his prospective in-laws regard warnings of judgment as a joke, however (vv. 12–14).

Maybe Lot is not too sure himself about what his visitors say. At any rate, when morning comes he has done nothing. Further urging meets no response, and so he and his immediate family forcibly receive a merciful expulsion (vv. 15–16). Even then Lot dithers and haggles and, astonishingly, is allowed to go to Zoar rather than the hills (vv. 17–23), although just as Sodom is turning out not to be the paradise that Lot originally imagined, Zoar will be no lasting refuge either (v. 30).

Disaster then comes upon the whole region. Lot's wife, whose looking back is perhaps to be imagined as lingering behind, becomes like one of the figures discovered in Pompeii (vv. 24–26). The region so desolate that it becomes known as the Dead Sea is to be envisaged as a picture of God's judgment on human corruption.

Abraham sees the desolation. His response is not recounted, yet the narrator makes clear that the mercy received by Lot in the midst of judgment is somehow because of Abraham. Abraham's probing engagement with God is a kind of intercessory prayer (vv. 27–29).

4 Puzzling integrity

Genesis 20:1–18

In some ways Abraham is a very slow learner. He repeats the lie about Sarah that he earlier perpetrated upon Pharaoh (vv. 1–2), only this time it is more serious, for this is the time in which Sarah is destined to become pregnant with Abraham's child. Drastic measures are called for, and so God speaks to Abimelech (vv. 3–7).

The conversation is intriguing. Abimelech is in danger of death (vv. 3, 7), yet Abimelech speaks to God with the same kind of concern for justice that earlier marked Abraham (v. 4; cf. 18:25). Abimelech has been deceived by both Abraham and Sarah, and has acted unwittingly. God grants this, and indeed it was because of Abimelech's integrity that God kept him from sinning. Abimelech has acted with more integrity than Abraham, yet his near-adultery is a moral offence that requires intercessory prayer on the part of the less-than-honest Abraham. (Abraham is called a prophet only in the sense that he is someone who intercedes with God, for intercession was one of the responsibilities of a prophet: cf. 1 Samuel 12:23; Jeremiah 27:18.) Although, generally speaking, authentic prayer requires openness and integrity before God, the people of God may yet be obligated to pray even when their living is no better, and possibly worse, than that of those for whom they pray.

Next day Abimelech issues a stinging rebuke to Abraham (vv. 8–9), and then asks what on earth moved him to act in such a way (v. 10). Abraham pleads first that he thought there was no 'fear of God' in the place (v. 11). The person who fears God is one who, among other things, does not take advantage of the weak and vulnerable (cf. Leviticus 19:14; Deuteronomy 25:17–18). Abraham had feared that, as a resident alien, he would be picked off by ruthless people. Yet the story shows how mistaken Abraham was, for Abimelech acted with more integrity than he did: not all foreigners are like the inhabitants of Sodom.

Abraham's second excuse is that he was not really telling a lie anyway, for Sarah is his half-sister (vv. 12–13). One presumes that here

Abraham is telling the truth, though the narrative does not specify.

Abimelech responds with generous reparations (vv. 14, 16) and a gracious offer (v. 15). God's response to Abraham's prayer leaves Abimelech and his family healthy and fertile (vv. 17–18). God's commitment to Abraham makes Abraham a blessing in some rather strange ways.

5 Laughter and life

Genesis 21:1–21

At long last, almost beyond hope, God's promise is fulfilled. A son is born to Abraham and Sarah. A sense of joy is apparent in the repeated reference to things happening as the Lord had said (vv. 1–2). Although previously both Abraham and Sarah had laughed in incredulity at God's promise, now Sarah laughs with the laughter of sheer wonderment, which is only disbelieving in the sense that it all seems too good to be true. All these different laughters are commemorated in the name of their son, for the Hebrew form of Isaac, *yitshaq*, means simply 'he/one laughs'. Joy seems complete.

The joy lasts for perhaps two or three years, which is the common length of time for the weaning of children in antiquity. Since the first years of a child's life are also the most perilous for its survival, by the time a child is being weaned there is every reason to expect that it will survive into adulthood. So weaning would be an appropriate occasion for a celebratory feast (v. 8).

But there is a fly in the ointment (v. 9). Hagar's earlier return to her mistress was presumably as displeasing in its own way to Sarah as it was to Hagar. The precise reason for Sarah's displeasure with Ishmael is, however, unclear. The NRSV text, following the ancient Greek and Latin versions, has Ishmael playing/laughing with Isaac, which could be entirely innocent. The point then would be Sarah's sense of her own previous blunder: having helped to bring about Ishmael's birth, she now sees an innocent Ishmael as a threat to Isaac's being the heir to his father. But the shorter Hebrew text, in NRSV footnote, suggests a different scenario: the Hebrew uses another form of the verb 'laugh' (*metsahek*), which on its own in this context would naturally bear a negative connotation—that is, 'mocking'. To be sure, Sarah's behaviour is on any reckoning mean, but she may have been prompted by the son's taking after the mother in displaying scorn.

God overrules a distressed Abraham, because Ishmael also will become the ancestor of a people (vv. 11–13). Hagar goes off with Ishmael, clearly not knowing where to go or what to do, which is why she readily despairs (vv. 14–16). But God comes and promises life, a life symbolized by the water that is instantly discovered. Hereafter, the wilderness, which had initially been a place of apparent death, becomes a place of life (vv. 17–21).

6 The supreme trial

God speaks the unspeakable. Abraham is to take Isaac, the apple of his eye as well as the tangible fulfilment of God's promises, and reduce him to ashes and smoke as an offering to God (vv. 1–2).

How can this be? The narrator explains that this is a test (v. 1). Testing is a regular action of God to draw people out into a deeper obedience. In Deuteronomy 8, for example, God tests Israel in order to do them good (8:16), teaching them, through what they undergo, a basic truth about life (8:2–3). But a test may yet be demanding beyond imagination.

Although we may picture Abraham feeling bewilderment or resentment, the narrator tells us nothing of his feelings, only what Abraham does: he acts in obedience (vv. 3–6). Isaac's question is simple and poignant; Abraham's answer is equally simple and, whatever his possible feelings, expresses a fundamental trust in God (vv. 7–8).

Abraham presses on, and only at the last moment does the angel speak and stop him. He reveals the purpose of the test—to establish that Abraham truly 'fears God' (vv. 9–12). In the Old Testament, 'fearing God' is the prime term for appropriate human responsiveness to God (cf. Psalm 103:11, 13, 17; Luke 1:50). In Christian parlance, the story establishes that Abraham is a 'true believer'. It shows that true faith means faithfulness to God, even when that faithfulness is a path of incomprehension and darkness.

One immediate consequence is that Abraham is able to offer a ram instead of Isaac, and to celebrate God's provision in the name of the place (vv. 13–14). Where is the place? Verse 2 spoke of Moriah, and 2 Chronicles 3:1 speaks of Solomon building the temple on Mount Moriah—so Abraham's sacrifice is in the location of the Jerusalem temple. This suggests that his story may be meant to show the true meaning of worship in the temple: the offering of an animal is a true sacrifice when it represents the kind of total self-giving that characterizes Abraham.

God's promise of blessing is now renewed in glowing terms: Abraham's obedience will bring blessing to many (vv. 15–18).

Abraham's son has definitively been confirmed as the father of many. What remains is for the divine promise to be worked out in human terms. So amidst the genealogy that follows (vv. 20–24), we note the name of the woman who will one day become the mother of many—Rebekah.

Guidelines

Paul focuses on Abraham as the one who trusted and took God at his word, even when he had to hope against hope (Galatians 3; Romans 4). James focuses on Abraham as the one whose response to God was total and unreserved in what he did (James 2:18–24). Can we hold together 'faith' and 'works' so that our response to God can have something of the richness of Abraham's?

FURTHER READING

R.W.L. Moberly, 'Genesis 12—50', in John W. Rogerson, R.W.L. Moberly and William Johnstone, *Genesis and Exodus*, Sheffield Academic Press, 2001.

R.W.L. Moberly, 'Living Dangerously: Genesis 22 and the Quest for Good Biblical Interpretation', in Ellen F. Davis and Richard B. Hays (eds.), *The Art of Reading Scripture*, Eerdmans, 2003, pp.181–97.

Walter Brueggemann, *Genesis*, Interpretation Bible Commentary, John Knox Press, 1982.

Nahum Sarna, *Genesis*, JPS Torah Commentary, Jewish Publication Society, 1989.

Gordon Wenham, *Genesis 16—50*, Word Biblical Commentary 2, Word Books, 1994.

THE SONG OF SONGS

The Song of Songs, or Song of Solomon, is a celebration of human love between the sexes. It has over the centuries been allegorized to refer to the mutual love of God and Israel, but nowadays many readers prefer to take it at face value to refer to human relationship. The absence of reference to Yahweh in this work is notable. The Song is a series of love poems or songs that are unlikely to form a strict unity, but have been gathered together, possibly by sages who edited the work, or else in an oral folk tradition.

There are elements of dialogue in the Song, with both man and woman taking turns to be the speaker. In fact, somewhat surprisingly given the culture of the time, the woman speaks more than the man, and this has led some scholars to posit female authorship of the work. The authorship of the piece, however, is lost in the mists of time, unless one takes the superscription at face value and attributes the Song to Solomon's pen. The Rabbis did, and saw the Song as the work of the youthful Solomon, Proverbs as the product of his middle years and Ecclesiastes as the work of the old Solomon, tired with life.

In this week of St Valentine's day, it is appropriate to muse on the nature of human love, and it is in the Song of Songs that we find this little gem of celebration of the love of man and woman for each other.

1 Superscription and opening poem of admiration
Song of Songs 1:1–4

In the opening line we read the ascription to Solomon. Is this simply a traditional attribution, to be taken with a pinch of salt, or are we to ascribe any or all of the poem to Solomonic inspiration, if not to his pen? In Proverbs and Ecclesiastes we have similar attributions to Solomon, and those two works are wisdom literature, for which Solomon was famed. The Song of Songs is not usually classified as wisdom literature since its genre is that of love poetry, so the Solomonic attribution is clearly not for the same reasons, unless of course the work was edited by 'the wise' of Israel at some stage. The attribution could, then, be a later addition to try to ascribe authorship to an otherwise unconnected string of poems. However, there are five other references to Solomon in the work, as well as references to 'the king', who might also be identified with Solomon, so it seems as if the Solomonic connection is a little greater than just 1:1 would imply. Solomon seems more integral to the work. We will explore this further in other passages.

In verse 2 we are introduced to the woman, who speaks first of the love of her lover. He is described by her in terms of rich fragrances and described as popular among the maidens. Then, in verse 4, we are introduced to the character of 'the king'. Is this Solomon himself? Is he the same person as the lover described by the woman in the first two verses? Sometimes a bride and bridegroom are described as 'king' and 'queen' in a kind of role-play that indicates their specialness on their wedding day. Is that what we have here, and is the entering of the chambers a reference to the wedding night? There is a wider debate here about whether the couple are married or not, over which scholars vary in their opinion. It is not explicitly stated in the passage but if, for example, the sages edited the piece, they would not have approved of sexual love outside married confines (see the contrast between the loose woman of Proverbs 7 and Woman Wisdom who is identified with the figure of the good wife in Proverbs 8; cf. Proverbs 31).

In verse 4b we seem to have a chorus, as the person changes to 'we'. These are possibly the 'daughters of Jerusalem' mentioned later in the book, but it might be a literary technique used as a sounding board for the woman's emotions. The love of the pair seems here to be approved by the chorus, but then the last line, 'rightly do they love you', would seem to belong in the woman's mouth, speaking of the maidens' right to love the man. The woman is not deluded enough to think that she is the only one who admires him!

2 The woman describes herself and her lover

Song of Songs 1:5–8

In the second part of chapter 1 the woman describes herself as black and beautiful—like dark tents and costly curtains. We do not know whether she was black by race or simply because of the burning of her skin by the sun, although the latter is suggested in verse 6. For the first time she addresses the 'daughters of Jerusalem', who form a chorus, and asks not to be stared at because of her colour: this seems to be a sensitive point for her. Perhaps the daughters of Jerusalem, being city dwellers, would have had more refined skin.

Verse 6 brings a reference to the woman's 'mother's sons'. Oddly, there is no mention of her father anywhere in the Song, and these 'mother's sons' might be her half-brothers. They were, it seems, angry with her—because of her outdoor skin, perhaps? The reference to vineyards might suggest that she was so busy looking after others that she neglected her own person.

In verse 7, the woman turns to her lover, who is described here in pastoral terms that indicate a shepherd. She asks why she should be veiled—harking back again, it seems, to the comments about her dark skin—as his companions (the sheep) are not. This imagery could well be figurative, both in terms of the vineyard and the flocks. We could posit a shepherd figure as the lover here, and it has been suggested that we have a three-way plot in the Song, with king and shepherd vying for the love of the woman—but equally a royal figure can be portrayed in the Bible as a shepherd pasturing flocks (for example, David the shepherd-king; see also Ezekiel 34). In verse 8 we seem to have a response—possibly by the chorus—picking up the imagery of flocks and sheep. The injunction is to follow the tracks of the flock to find the shepherd.

3 The restless quest for the lover

Song of Songs 3:1–5

The woman often yearns for the man. In the opening verses of chapter 3 she describes her search for her man as she lies restlessly in bed. Some scholars have suggested that this is a regular dream, and that she only walks the streets in her dream, but we could take it literally—finding her lover gone, she goes in search of him. This is a similar image to that of Woman Wisdom in Proverbs 8, who walks the streets trying to find young men to listen to her words of wisdom, and to that of the loose woman who is her opposite, in Proverbs 7, who wanders from her house looking for men to lure to her bed.

The woman in the Song is tireless in her search, asking the sentinels who kept guard at night on the walls of a town or city if they have seen her lover. It is interesting that in this chapter we move from the pastoral context of sheep and vineyards to a town or city atmosphere. A hint of the desperation of romantic love accompanies this description: this has led some scholars to think that a married context for the lovers would be unlikely, because within marriage the relationship is more stable and predictable. When at last she finds her lover, the woman holds him tight. We then find a reference to the woman's mother's house (v. 4), one of a number of references to the woman's family, and this would more naturally suggest the home of an unmarried woman rather than a married one. However, it is interesting that she has no qualms about allowing her man into the very bedchamber in which she was conceived.

Verse 5 brings references to the daughters of Jerusalem, to whom much of the description is addressed. The woman swears by gazelles and wild doves—animals that are often used in descriptions of the beloved in the Song. It is perhaps surprising that she does not swear by Yahweh. She tells the chorus of women not to stir up love until the time is ripe. Perhaps she is feeling the intensity of desire that does not allow the soul to rest, possibly referring back to her restless quest for her lover earlier in the chapter. Strong yearning for a lover can create this situation of finding no satisfaction except in their company, and feeling a real sickness at being apart.

4 Solomon's wedding song

Song of Songs 3:6–11

In the second half of chapter 3 we have the famous description of Solomon's litter (or palanquin) appearing as if from nowhere, like a caravan from the desert. This links the Song closely to Solomon. The richness of the description comes across strongly, and there is no doubt that royalty is being described here. The sense of smell is aroused, as well as it being a splendid sight for the eyes. The column of smoke (v. 6) may well be the smoke of burning incense. Myrrh and frank-incense were precious perfumes, imported from abroad, and the 'fragrant powders' probably refer to spices or other perfumes from the East. This is a great procession, 60 men flanking the litter, each armed to defend the king (particularly at night, when bandits might roam).

Verses 9–10 provide a rich description of the palanquin, which is most likely a covered litter, although a covered sedan chair has also been suggested. It is made from the best wood—the cedars of Lebanon. It is then flanked with precious metals and fine royal purple coverings (cloth dyed with reddish purple from the shells of molluscs found on the Phoenician coast). We are told that its interior was 'inlaid with love': this may refer to the way the palanquin was put together—in a loving fashion—or perhaps the image is designed to pick up the mood of the desire of the lovers for each other.

At the end of the passage, the daughters of Jerusalem are enjoined to appear to look at the king in his splendour. The 'daughters of Zion' are probably the same group by another name—Zion, the holy temple mount, being representative of the city of Jerusalem. These women are adjured to look at Solomon's crown, and again we have a reference to a mother, this time Solomon's. The women take important roles in this Song. The crown may be a garland worn especially for a wedding, and the next line suggests that this is in fact the context. Solomon has arrived to claim his bride: this is his wedding day! We might compare Psalm 45:10–15 for a similar description of a monarch's wedding. This descrip-tion could well be an old one, which could even go back to the time of Solomon, and this is perhaps the strongest evidence alongside the super-scription for a more than superficial connection of the Song to Solomon, the wisest king of Israel. If not an authorial link, there is clearly a traditional link coming through here and at other key points in the Song.

5 The man's turn to admire

Song of Songs 4:1–7

Although there are more words from the woman than the man in the Song, that is not to suggest that the love is one-sided. In this passage we find a description by the man of the beauty of the woman. The repetition of 'how beautiful' at the beginning denotes the man's passionate excitement for his beloved. Clearly, it is chiefly her physical appearance that delights him, although this is not a superficial admiration, for other words suggest that he is in love with the whole person, not just with her looks.

In this passage, the woman is described as wearing a veil, whereas earlier in the Song, as we have seen, her skin is dark and she appears to have been burnt by the sun. The man uses a good deal of animal imagery in his description of the woman, imagery that sounds odd to our ears. So her eyes are like doves behind her veil. Her hair is likened to a flock of goats going down a slope—a flowing and rippling movement. The description passes from eyes and hair to teeth, which are likened to shorn ewes that are washed—hence white teeth. The reference to the ewes bearing twins and not being bereaved (v. 2) is an odd one: many scholars have taken it to mean that the teeth are in pairs and none is missing, or maybe there is a deliberate double meaning here, both images in any case representing perfection. In ancient times, people would have kept their teeth for a good deal less time than we do, so a full set of teeth might well be worthy of comment!

The man's attention moves to her lips and mouth, to her cheeks, which are like a ripe pomegranate—sweet and red—and then to her neck, which is described as like the tower of David, Israel's greatest king. It is clearly a strong and long neck! Just as weapons hang from the tower, so presumably jewellery hangs at her neck. It is interesting that we again find overtones of royalty in the description. We should remember also that the woman's features are behind a veil, so presumably some of the fanciful imagination of the lover is coming into play.

As attention moves to the breasts (v. 5), again animal imagery is used, this time of fawns and gazelles, and in verse 6 we find rich myrrh and frankincense again. The beloved is flawless: words almost fail the lover, so overwhelmed is he.

6 Abstract musing on love and Solomon's vineyard

Verses 6b–7 are distinctive as they are the only abstract musing on the nature of love in the whole Song. In the rest of the poem, love is celebrated in the context of two specific people's love for each other. Love is described here as strong as death, with the inference that not even death can conquer it. It is as powerful as a raging flame. It cannot be drowned and it cannot be bought—in fact, any attempt to buy it would be rejected out of hand. The images increase in power—from strength to relentlessness to vehemence. Scholars have argued that these two verses are possibly a later addition by the sages, who wished to broaden the context out from just the love of an individual man and woman. This would have had the effect of putting the Song of Songs in a wider wisdom context, which would reflect more generally on human nature and relationships (cf. Proverbs 5:15–19; 30:19). This might explain the Solomonic link, at least in part.

In verses 8–9 we seem to have the introduction of new speakers, who are possibly the woman's brothers. The mention of her lacking breasts suggests that she is young and virginal, so maybe this is a flashback to her youth. The brothers protect their young sister at all costs. The imagery of a wall and door are used: the brothers will reinforce such battlements with rich metals or woods, in echoes of the luxurious language that we have already heard in reference to Solomon. In verse 10, the woman picks up the wall imagery, possibly answering her brothers. She is strong enough to take care of herself—she is a grown woman now. She is not threatening; she brings peace to her lover.

In verses 11–12 Solomon reappears, this time described in the third person. His vineyard is mentioned, along with the wealth it gives him (Baal-hamon means 'possessor of wealth', as well as possibly indicating a real place where a vineyard was to be found). Some scholars suggest that the vineyard is representative of Solomon's harem, and this is in contrast to the woman's own vineyard—presumably her lover. If Solomon is indeed the lover, it may indicate a comparison between Solomon's wealth and the woman's love for him. This, in the harem context, might suggest a special relationship for her with the king outside more official contexts. If the lover is another person (possibly 'the shepherd' mentioned earlier in the Song), then a contrast would be being made here between Solomon's wealth and 'the beloved', who might well be poor. This is poetry, and sometimes a clear sense is impossible to find: why the keepers of the fruit of the vineyard and their wages would be mentioned in this context is a mystery, unless it is just poetic licence to embellish the image further!

Guidelines

The Song of Songs is the only text in the Bible that openly and unreservedly celebrates the love of two people for each other. It doesn't presuppose any moral context: even the married context is a moot point. It is open, explicit at times and always celebratory. Like love itself, it lifts the spirits and makes life worth living. It is fascinating that such a book exists in holy scripture, indicating a joy in the wonder of being human, itself implicitly seen as God-given. We hear a good deal in today's society about love: we hear of long-term loyal relationships, of people who are in and out of relationships, of young people searching for love and finding it hard to pin down; we hear of the passion of a first embrace and of the excitement of new love. All these different aspects of love are reflected in the Song. We find longing, seeking, admiring and a wedding. We find musings on the nature of love and its enduring strength. On Valentine's day there is an opportunity to remind our own 'beloved' of our sustained love, or indeed there is a chance to indicate to an unsuspecting person that he or she is admired from afar! Although the modern St Valentine's day may to a certain extent be a creation of the card and flower shops, it does celebrate an essential part of human existence—many think it the most important aspect of life—and it reminds us not to take love for granted, at whatever stage of life and love we may be.

FURTHER READING

A. Bloch and C. Bloch, *The Song of Songs: A New Translation*, University of California Press, 1995.

R.E. Murphy, *The Song of Songs* (Hermeneia), Fortress Press, 1990.

R. Gordis, *The Song of Songs and Lamentations*, KTAV, 1974.

ROMANS 7—16

Before Christmas we studied the first six chapters of Romans. There we met a Paul obsessed by the gospel, which he described as 'the power of God for salvation to everyone who has faith' (1:16). Everyone needs this gospel, regardless of what 'group' they belong to (such as Jew or Gentile or their modern equivalents), and everyone has equal access to it, through faith in Jesus. The power of God is available to everyone without distinction. Such a message, though, created its own problems. For example, does this gospel message mean that God has abandoned his promises to the Jewish people? Has he moved the goalposts? If Jesus' death on the cross has saved us, does it matter if we continue doing wrong?

Over the next three weeks, we will read together the rest of Romans (chs. 7—16). In the first half (until the end of ch. 11), Paul continues to wrestle with the different aspects of his gospel message and the problems that it might appear to raise. This highlights that it is no good for us to 'proclaim the gospel' glibly, thinking that its wisdom is immediately self-evident and that queries about it are mere excuses. Paul takes these apparent problems seriously. In the final quarter of the letter (chs. 12—16) Paul turns to the impact that his gospel message should have in practical living. Theology that makes no different in practice is bad theology.

Quotations are taken from the New Revised Standard Version.

1 Is God's law good or bad?

Romans 7:1–14

The good news, says Paul, is that we are no longer imprisoned in a world in which we desperately try to get things right but never manage it. Through what Jesus has done, 'now we are discharged from the law, dead to that which held us captive' (v. 6). In verses 1–3, Paul justifies his logic. In any legal system, law affects you only while you are alive; marriage lasts only 'until death us do part'. An action that would be adultery if your partner were still alive is perfectly acceptable once he or she has died. Death changes everything. So too with us: our participation in Jesus' death (see 6:1–8) means that everything has changed. Our old marriage to the law has been broken; our new marriage with Jesus through the Spirit can begin: 'you have died to the law… so that you may belong to another' (v. 4).

However, the law we are talking about here is not some law made by an evil tyrant, but God's own law given to the Jewish people. Does it make sense to say that God's law had such a bad effect that Jesus needed to come to set people free from it? Is the law a bad thing?

'No,' says Paul categorically (vv. 7, 12, 13). The law itself is a good thing, but it was used by sin to produce a bad outcome. The twists and turns of Paul's argument can be hard to follow. The main point is clear, though. The law was good but limited—it pointed out good from evil ('I would not have known…', v. 7; '… might be shown to be sin', v. 13) but didn't help to achieve the good. Furthermore, once God's law has been revealed to us, it is somehow even worse when we then don't do it. The law itself cannot be faulted—it truly revealed God's will—but when combined with our sinfulness a negative result is produced. Thus, sin killed me through the commandment (v. 11).

Sadly, many of us recognize this situation. Knowledge of good and evil does not bring the ability to get our behaviour right. God's high standards applied to weak humans bring slavery and death if they are not coupled with the forgiveness and power that come through Jesus. Too often we behave as if, as we know the rules, we should be able to keep them in our own strength. Or worse still, we demand this of others. Let us remember that however good, just and holy the rules are, rules themselves never bring life.

2 Struggling with sin

Romans 7:14–25

This passage, in which Paul describes an inner battle between the desire to do good and the reality of doing evil, has given rise to two different interpretations which have battled it out throughout Christian history. The key question is: who is the 'I' here? More precisely, does this passage describe the life of a person without Jesus or the life of a Christian?

Various features of the passage point to it being the description of life without Jesus. It follows on naturally from the previous passage, with the good news waiting until 8:1 ('there is therefore now no condemnation'). Furthermore, the whole tone just seems too negative: 'I do not do what I want' (v. 15), 'nothing good dwells within me' (v. 18), 'captive to the law of sin' (v. 23). In particular, can the Christian be said to be 'sold into slavery under sin' (v. 14)?

Throughout history, however, many commentators have connected this passage to the experience of the Christian believer, for the simple and rather compelling reason that it seems to fit the reality of our lives. 'I do not do the good I want, but the evil I do not want is what I do' (v. 19) is certainly often my experience. Some have also doubted that Paul could apply 'I delight in the law of God in my inmost self' (v. 22) to those he has earlier called 'enemies' of God (5:10), although this is to overlook the fact that all people have been created in God's image and at some level yearn for him.

On balance, it seems that Paul is describing the struggle of the pious person attempting to do good, battling against the slavery to sin, without the release and power that Jesus brings. But what do we make of the fact that it so often fits our lives too? The answer is that we are only halfway there. In the language of Romans 6:5, we *have* died and we *will be* resurrected. We live in an in-between phase: we are now set free from sin, but still drawn to it. This tension will be explored further in chapter 8. For now, we can recognize the genuine desire of many around us to do good, even if alone we can never break our bondage to sin. And we can rejoice that Jesus does rescue us from the never-ending struggle (vv. 24–25). We will not be completely rid of the struggle until our own resurrection, but this is no excuse for continual failure to do good in our lives. If our rescue by Jesus is to mean anything, it should be beginning to change our daily actions and thoughts right now.

3 The work of the Spirit

Romans 8:1–17

After the struggle and difficulty of chapter 7, it is good news to hear the words of chapter 8:1: 'There is… no condemnation for those who are in Christ Jesus.' Verse 3 explains why. The law was weak, as we have seen in chapter 7: it could point out good and evil, but it could not break human tendency to do evil, nor give humans the power to do good. Something more, something different was needed. 'God has done what the law… could not do: by sending his own Son… to deal with sin.' Jesus dealt with sin. The law and our own human strivings could never manage this, but Jesus has done it.

What God has done is not a reversal of the law, though, as if God has changed how people should live. On the contrary, God has acted so that the good which the law always marked out can now actually be achieved (v. 4). How? Because now we 'walk… according to the Spirit' (v. 4). This combination is important. We cannot get anywhere without the freedom that comes from what God has done in Jesus. But neither can we just accept that and get on with life on our own. For our ongoing life to stay on course, we need God's Spirit.

Verses 5–13 depict a continuing tension. Although we are now set free from bondage to sin, we are not yet set free from the possibility of it. We have a daily choice to set our mind on either 'the things of the flesh' or 'of the Spirit'. However, such a tension will not last for ever. Jesus' resurrection from the dead makes it clear that we too will finally one day be resurrected (v. 11); we will finally be released from those thoughts, desires and inclinations that are alien to God. Note also how this final release is described, as the time when God 'will give life to your mortal bodies' (v. 11). Our future hope is not for the escape of our 'souls' from the 'prison of the body' as many people think. No, the future hope is that our human bodies might be transformed ('resurrected') so that we can live lives fully pleasing to God. This theme of the transformation of the physical world is picked up in the next reading.

Finally, Paul gives confirmation of this future hope (vv. 14–17). The fact that we already call God our father testifies to the fact that we are his children, and thus that we share in Jesus' status. Jesus himself suffered, so our present sufferings shouldn't make us doubt the future; but Jesus was then resurrected and glorified, and we too will share his glory. As we rejoice in the certainty of this future hope, we must ask God to show us in what areas of our lives we continue to 'set our mind on the flesh', and instead invite his Spirit to guide and empower us.

4 All creation will be renewed

There is more. It is not just we humans who are caught in this tension, longing for the future transformation but having to live in the present. Creation itself is caught in the same tension: 'the whole creation has been groaning in labour pains until now; and not only the creation, but we ourselves' (vv. 22–23). (Note the image of labour pains, often used in the Bible to describe this tension: the pain currently is very, very bad, but at the end there is something very, very good, which makes it all worthwhile.)

The scope of Paul's thought here is huge: the gospel is not just a concern for humanity but for the whole of creation. Indeed, the whole of creation is tied up in our fate: 'the creation waits with eager longing for the revealing of the children of God' (v. 19). If Christianity often seems individualistic, this is our fault, not Paul's—he has a far bigger vision.

The logic behind Paul's argument comes from Genesis 1–3. At the very beginning, before humans turned away from God, humanity was given a task from God. God created the garden, but humanity was told to 'till it and keep it' (Genesis 2:15). God rules the whole world but he 'sub-contracted' that rule to humanity: 'Be fruitful and multiply, and fill the earth and subdue it; and have dominion…' (Genesis 1:28). Unfortunately, humanity turned away from God, and so rather than 'keeping' the creation and ruling it in the generous, life-enhancing way that God rules, we turned this superiority to exploitation. Our sin damaged the whole creation. We were created to be the gardeners— without us, the garden has become overgrown and out of control.

The language of 'dominion' in relation to the environment raises concerns for many. When we look around our world, however, we have to admit that the biblical picture is true. We do have control of our world: it is we humans who have the power to destroy everything, from our neighbourhoods to the whole world. The problem does not come from admitting the truth that we have this dominion but from how we use it. The good news, says Paul, is that as we obtain the 'freedom of the glory of the children of God' creation itself will be set free (v. 21) from the evil that we brought to it by our rebellion against God. If this is true, then as we now seek to live by the Spirit, we should seek to have this role of 'God's gardeners'. In our choices, in our lifestyles and in our work, are we working with God's creation, bringing good out of it, or exploiting it for our own ends?

5 Security in God

Romans 8:24–39

Paul anticipates that these last chapters might leave us feeling bewildered. It would have been nicer to be told that everything has been achieved already, that Christians are free from sin and the created world is in harmony with the creator. Nicer but, in the real world, palpably false. Instead, Paul has painted a picture of life in the 'in-between times': we have been set free from bondage to sin, but can still do it; we now have life in the Spirit, but can still set our minds on the flesh; creation is still groaning, longing for change.

Such a picture has the great strength of tallying with the life we know. However, it can seem to undermine our confidence. This is not Paul's purpose. Now, as he reaches the end of his main presentation of the gospel message (chs. 1—8), he returns to the issue of the confidence we can have in what God has done. The current time of tension will bring suffering and groaning—there is no getting round that. What we hope for has not yet arrived (vv. 24–25). But three things ease this tension.

First, 'the Spirit helps us in our weakness' (v. 26). We are not left to survive these 'in-between times' ourselves. The Spirit understands our desires and longings. Even when we fail and turn back to the flesh, the Spirit knows that this is the result of our weakness, not our desire, and intercedes for us. We are not alone: God's Spirit himself is working in us, strengthening and caring for us.

Second, God's purposes cannot be thwarted (vv. 28–30). Those whom God has chosen he will not abandon, and will bring them through to the end. We misinterpret Paul here if we see this as saying that there is a group of people whom God has *not* chosen, who therefore never have any hope. Paul has been clear so many times that the gospel is open to everyone. On the contrary, his point is that our belonging to God's family does not depend on something as flimsy as our decision or our success; it is rooted in God's purposes, and so cannot fail.

Third, let's be sensible: if God, the creator of the whole world, is on our side, what do we actually expect to defeat us? (vv. 31–39). There is nothing in creation that can condemn those whom God forgives. There is no power in creation that can reverse God's will. The gospel is power for salvation, and nothing can overcome it. We can have full confidence in God as we live through 'the sufferings of this present time' (8:18).

6 But has the word of God failed?

Romans 9:1–29

The end of Romans 8 brought an end to Paul's main presentation of the gospel message. Therefore it might seem strange to 'tack on' this first part of Romans 9 at the end of this week's readings. However, doing this highlights to us the continued flow of the letter. Romans 9—11, often seen as a separate part of the letter, dealing with 'the problem of Israel', is in fact a necessary continuation from chapters 1—8. Paul's message is that 'the righteousness of God has been disclosed… for all who believe. For there is no distinction' (3:21–22), and at various points we have seen Paul trying to answer a charge that this means God has changed his mind and has abandoned his promises to the Jewish people. Now this issue becomes crucial, and becomes relevant to us. The end of chapter 8 has gloried in the fact that God's plans will be fulfilled, and that nothing can prevent this, but does not the history of Israel prove the opposite? Has the word of God to them failed (v. 6)? If so, might it fail to us as well? Is our confidence misplaced? The way God has treated his people in the past is crucial for us, who claim to be his people today.

Three things emerge from this passage. First, we must take seriously Paul's anguish in verses 1–5. He believes that his 'kindred according to the flesh' (that is, the Jewish people) are now in a terrible position. Their lack of acceptance of God's Messiah (who indeed emerged from them, v. 5) is not a trivial matter. Second (vv. 6–13), he challenges the idea that mere physical descent ever made anyone part of God's people, and here he returns to the arguments of chapter 2. This is the root of the problem for his Jewish compatriots. Their belief that physical descent from Abraham makes them part of the people of God by right is contradicted by the Old Testament itself (notice how John the Baptist made the same point, Matthew 3:9). God is not abandoning his people, but some who thought they had the right to be his people are sadly mistaken. Third (vv. 24–29), going on from this second point, there is no cause for complaint if God chose to include in the people of God some who were not physical descendents from Abraham. This is no novelty, but is contained in the Old Testament as well. The argument about the potter (vv. 14–23), with its implications of predestination, seem to sit uncomfortably with Paul's main point that the gospel is for everyone who believes. However, its main point is clear: it is foolish for us to argue that God must keep to the definitions of his people that we would like.

God's promise to his people has not failed; therefore, we who are his people now can have confidence in him. However, there is a warning here. Do we try to define the boundaries of God's people, or do we accept that that is God's job?

Guidelines

This week, our readings have depicted the huge sweep of God's plan. We have, in effect, gone from creation through fall and salvation to the renewal of creation. Within all this, we find ourselves at a crucial moment. Through Jesus Christ, God has set us free from the wretched situation of aiming to do right but always ending up doing wrong, where 'I'm only human' means 'I can't get it right'. The law (and indeed all 'rules') merely highlights the problem; the solution comes in Jesus and in the Spirit living within us.

The end has not yet come, however. We still live with a struggle: we are no longer in bondage to sin, but we are still drawn to it. Often, people fall into one of two errors. Either they forget that something has happened or they forget that something more is still to come. Which way do you lean? Do you live as if what Jesus has done, and the presence of the Spirit, does not really make much difference in the daily grind? Did Romans 7:14–25 sound like your life? Or do you live as if everything has already been achieved, that there is no future trans-formation, and that sin and difficulty now, whether in yourself or in others, is an affront—a denial of the Christian message or, perhaps, proof that Paul's claims for the gospel are excessive? Being caught in this mid-point, this period of tension, is not always easy. Pray that God would show you which error you might fall into, and that he would give you a new vision of his amazing plan.

1 The way to God

Romans 9:30—10:13

The problem, says Paul, is that his Jewish compatriots have been seeking God in the wrong way. The description he gives is tragic. There is no doubting that they have been striving for righteousness (9:31) and have a true zeal for God (10:2). If they had been wicked, godless people, somehow their mistake would not seem so bad, but they are not. Their zeal is not in doubt; the problem is that they are ignorant of God's way of righteousness (10:3). They have been trying to reach God, to please God, in the wrong way—striving as if righteousness was based on works, not faith (9:32); effectively setting up their own system of righteousness rather than following God's (10:3).

Once again, we must take seriously Paul's anguish in verse 1 (similar to that in 9:1–5): he longs that salvation might come to them. Presumably, here Paul is not motivated just by national loyalties and love. He also must be conscious that the description he has given fitted his own life exactly (cf. Galatians 1:13–15; Philippians 3:4–6) until his vision of Jesus on the Damascus road. He hopes that God would rescue them like he did him.

Paul sees this situation as a fulfilment of Old Testament prophecies concerning Jerusalem, bringing together Isaiah 8:14 and Isaiah 28:16 (9:32–33), texts which are also used in the Gospels (e.g. Matthew 21:42) and in 1 Peter 2:6–8. These quotations from the Old Testament are important in Paul's continuing case that, while what he is preaching might seem new, it is in keeping with the Old Testament (cf. Romans 3:21). More particularly, though, they highlight how the very same thing—'the stone'—can be both the cause of stumbling for some and salvation for others. (For a Hebrew or Aramaic speaker, the point is particularly interesting, because the Hebrew/Aramaic for 'stone' is very similar to the word for 'son': they stumble over or believe in the son.) Jesus is both the cause of salvation for many and the one thing that others cannot accept.

Jesus has brought to an end any suggestion that works done according to the law are the entry criteria into God's people (10:4). This was never actually God's way of righteousness (as he demonstrated in Romans 4 from the example of Abraham), but now all is made clear. And the reason is simple: accessibility. Faith in Jesus is available to all. There is no need for someone to travel the heavens searching for God (10:6–8); there is no need to belong to a particular group ('there is no distinction', 10:12). All that is needed is belief, confessing that Jesus is Lord and calling on his name (10:4, 9–11, 13).

The tragedy Paul outlines continues today: Jesus, the one who brings salvation, is a stumbling-block to many—not so much to wicked people, but to earnest, pious people who can't manage to give up their own search for God and believe in Jesus. We should share Paul's anguish here, aware that we could easily be in the same situation, and we should ensure that we do not cloud the message of God's accessibility. Do we by our words and deeds suggest that more is needed than belief in Jesus?

2 The remnant

Romans 10:14—11:10

Paul continues to be troubled about his compatriots. The tragedy seems so great. Perhaps the problem is that they have not heard the message— it is not that they have rejected what God is doing, but just that they haven't heard about it. But no, Paul admits, through a series of steps and more Old Testament quotations (10:14–21). God has sent messengers to Israel, but the messengers have often not been listened to. Isaiah himself said as much (10:16, quoting Isaiah 53:1; 10:21, quoting Isaiah 65:1). The problem is not that God hasn't bothered to inform his people; the problem is in the fact that 'not all have obeyed the good news' (10:16; 'good news' here could be translated 'gospel').

Here at the end of chapter 10 Paul reaches his most negative conclusion. For all his anguish (9:1–5; 10:1–2), for all his defence of the advantages of 'the Jew' (3:1–2) and the goodness of the law (7:7–14), it almost seems as if God's ancestral people have 'failed to obtain what it was seeking' (11:7), that God has rejected his people (11:1) and thus that the 'word of God has failed' (9:6). Even if the problem is people's own unwillingness to follow what God is doing, this would still be a terrible conclusion, not only for those involved but also for us as we contemplate this great reversal.

But this is not a true analysis of the situation, Paul declares ('By no means!' 11:1). Many Jewish people have believed—take Paul himself, for example (11:1). The seemingly negative material in chapter 10 has been about the people taken as a whole, but within this wider body there is a 'remnant' who have believed. The idea of a remnant draws once more on the Old Testament. When Elijah despaired with God (just as Paul himself has been wrestling in anguish), he was told that while it was true that many in Israel had turned to Baal, not all had. The remnant remained (1 Kings 19:1–18). The same is true in his day, Paul suggests (11:5). Indeed, this is really going back to the argument he made at the beginning of chapter 9: 'not all of Abraham's children are his true descendants' (9:7).

Once again, these passages remind us of how grateful we should be to God that his grace reached us. Through all this human rebellion and turning away, of which we are equally guilty, he nevertheless found us, just as he did Paul on the Damascus road. We should also be humble as we read this tragic history. Confidence is right, as Paul expounded in Romans 8:28–29, but we must also ensure that we as individuals and in our churches 'obey the good news' (10:16) and do not become 'disobedient and contrary people' (10:21).

3 All Israel will be saved

Romans 11:11–36

Paul is not yet satisfied with his explanation. 'So is that it?' he can hear his Gentile readers thinking. 'All but a remnant from Israel have now fallen, and apart from them God's purposes have now flowed to the Gentiles?'

'No,' Paul replies firmly (v. 11: 'by no means'; v. 29: 'the gifts and the calling of God are irrevocable'). There is nothing necessarily permanent about the current situation. This could well be a step in God's plan: the 'full inclusion' of Israel may well be around the corner (v. 12).

Paul then provides an image of God's people (vv. 13–24), attempting to summarize his whole argument, which we can note is addressed particularly to Gentiles (v. 13). The people of God are like an olive tree. Israel are the roots and the natural branches. Gentile believers in Rome or elsewhere must not become arrogant (vv. 19–21). While it is true that some of the natural branches have been broken off ('because of their unbelief', v. 20) and Gentile wild branches have been grafted in (v. 17), there need be nothing permanent about this situation. Wild branches could easily be removed (v. 21) and natural branches added back in (vv. 23–24, 'if they do not persist in unbelief'). Indeed, it would be particularly easy to add natural branches back, because 'by nature' they belong to the olive tree, unlike the 'grafted in' wild branches.

There are two crucial points here. First, the roots are Israel; the natural branches are Israel. There remains a special status, which the Gentile believers would do well to remember. God has not abandoned his ancestral people. Second, all the grafting in or breaking off is on the grounds of belief.

Paul's conclusion, 'And so all Israel will be saved' (v. 26), has been interpreted in different ways. Some see it as a declaration that, in the end, all the natural branches will be grafted back in, that all the Jewish people will be saved. This would indeed be a mystery (11:25) and the cause of great wonder and praise (11:33–36). Others feel that this outcome is unlikely, for it appears to contradict what Paul has said earlier that 'not all Israelites truly belong to Israel' (9:6). Following after the olive tree illustration, perhaps 'all Israel' means 'the whole tree'. The whole of this 'renewed' Israel will be saved, perhaps the whole of 'true Israel', which is based on the Jewish people and includes many of them, but from which some have been broken off and other Gentiles added in.

Either way, what is clear here is that there is no 'second way' to God: there is only one 'olive tree'. Throughout Romans in almost every passage, Paul has argued that 'there is no distinction'—everyone comes to God through faith in Jesus—and that whatever 'group' you belong to cannot change this. The natural branches grafted back on to the tree were done so because of faith. Indeed, in his quotation from Isaiah 59:20, the 'Deliverer' can be nobody else but Jesus (v. 26).

We should heed Paul's warning against arrogance, thinking that we have a right to be part of God's people when we are really just the recipients of God's mercy. And we can join with Paul in wondering about God's amazing plan.

4 One body

Romans 12:1–8

Finally, Paul has come to the end of this theological outline of the gospel and the difficult issues it raises, and can turn to the effect it has on daily life. However, we have deliberately not chosen to begin a new week in *Guidelines* at the beginning of chapter 12, for we should not think of theology and practical life as two different components which can be dealt with separately in our lives. They are the two sides of the same coin. Indeed, Paul links them closely together here in verses 1–2.

First (v. 1), he appeals to the Romans 'by the mercies of God' or perhaps 'in view of God's mercy' (NIV). If you were hearing the letter read out at one sitting in the Roman church, it would be impossible to hear this phrase without thinking of all that has been explained in the previous eleven chapters. Paul does not say that because of what God has done we must live ethical lives, as if we somehow have to earn our place among God's people by our righteousness. It is an appeal, in effect saying, 'Given all this, how can you do anything other than present your bodies to God?' A better understanding of what God has done (chs. 1—11) should result in a different way of life. Also, note here how language that seems appropriate to the temple ('sacrifice', 'holy', 'worship') is now applied to ethics for life: God is in the world, not a building.

Second (v. 2), Paul links our conduct with the 'renewing of our minds'. In the battle to avoid being conformed to the standards of behaviour of those around us, but instead to live out God's will (in the language of 8:1–13, living 'according to the Spirit', not 'according to the flesh'), changed minds are crucial. Understanding better what God has done will allow us more easily to determine what God would have us do in any given situation.

The point of the next part (vv. 3–6) is straightforward but often neglected: the 'one body' of the Christian community is made up of different individuals, each with their own gifts to contribute (Paul gives the same teaching in more detail in 1 Corinthians 12). Paul's concern here seems to be that some people overestimate their own importance ('do not think of yourself more highly than you ought to', v. 3). The reverse is also possible: many people underestimate what God has given them, and therefore keep their gifts from being helpful to the wider church. Either is problematic.

5 Genuine love

Romans 12:9–21

Suddenly in this section, we have a string of commands and instructions rather than the detailed explanations and reasoning that make up the rest of the letter. Many scholars believe that Paul is here quoting some primitive Christian ethical code. Verses 9–13 certainly give an interesting 'rule of life', and verses 14–21 almost seem to be an exposition of Jesus' teaching in Matthew 5:38–47 (although Paul would have known it from oral tradition, since Matthew's Gospel would not have been written yet).

We noted that the previous passage was in effect a shortened version of 1 Corinthians 12; this passage, with its exposition of genuine love, is similar to 1 Corinthians 13. Later on, the discussion of food in Romans 14 has similarities with that in 1 Corinthians 8—10. These similarities probably reflect the fact that Paul's knowledge of the Roman church is limited, so his teaching here is what he expects will be appropriate for them, which not surprisingly means teaching similar to what he found necessary elsewhere (e.g. in Corinth).

Three particular points can be drawn from this passage. First, notice how the right responses to God, to 'one another' (i.e. other Christians), to outsiders and to external circumstances are all intermingled. There is no separation in the Christian life: everything arises out of the same process of 'being transformed by the renewal of our minds' (12:2). Second, at first glance there almost seems to be a contradiction between 'hate what is evil' (v. 9) and 'bless those who persecute you' (v. 14) or 'do not repay anyone evil for evil' (v. 17). The logic presumably is that evil itself should be 'hated'—shunned and avoided—but people who happen to be doing evil are a different matter. Paul himself must be conscious that he was a 'persecutor' before Jesus appeared to him: the persecution he instigated was evil, but he was still the object of God's blessing. Third, notice how Jesus himself embodied this teaching. Almost every phrase could be illustrated from Jesus' life, culminating in his overcoming of evil on the cross. As our minds are renewed, we are transformed into Jesus' image (2 Corinthians 3:18); we should have the same mind as was in Christ Jesus (Philippians 2:5).

6 Submission to authorities

Romans 13:1–7

Paul now turns from his general teaching on love to a particular, and more detailed, teaching on authorities. Indeed, this teaching on authorities then seems to feed into a specific issue or example of taxes (vv. 6–7): paying them was an issue of contention then, as now! This teaching does not find any parallels in 1 Corinthians, and was perhaps responding to some particular events or circumstances in the life of the Roman church.

Paul's teaching is clear, even if we find it troubling: 'those authorities that exist have been instituted by God' (v. 1). This is mainstream Jewish teaching derived from the belief in God's sovereignty—there is nothing in all of creation that can truly be outside God's control. Our attitude towards authority rather depends on where and when we are living. For those in modern Western societies, it is easy to assume that peace and security are natural, and to see governments as those interfering in our lives (and making us pay taxes!). This is a rather privileged standpoint. In Paul's day and, sadly, still for many today, disorder, crime and the collapse of justice into the 'rule of the jungle' are only a short step away. One only has to watch on TV the scenes in a major city where the government has collapsed—the looting, the fear and the destruction—

to realize that authority does in general restrain evil and bring about a situation in which one can 'live peaceably' (v. 18).

But what about when authorities go wrong? Jesus was unjustly killed. Paul himself was soon to be executed by the Roman authorities. The 20th century gave us enough examples of evil authorities. This other viewpoint is represented elsewhere in the New Testament, particularly in the book of Revelation. What seems a more balanced picture is given in 1 Peter 2—4, where Peter admits that Christians sometimes suffer not for doing evil but for doing good (1 Peter 3:14, 4:14), but nevertheless he urges them, 'For the Lord's sake, accept the authority of every human institution' (1 Peter 2:13).

These two viewpoints are not contradictory. Paul asserts that authorities in general are appointed by God for a good purpose. Throughout most of Romans, however, Paul has been explaining how far humans fall short of our calling and God's purpose (e.g. 7:19). Sadly, this can be equally true of authorities. We should pray for them.

Guidelines

This week, we have read the final parts of Paul's exposition of God's plan, with all its complexity, and seen him begin to outline the effect that this might have in daily life. Let us pause now to contemplate this some more. The idea can perhaps best be encapsulated in 12:2: 'Do not be conformed to this world, but be transformed by the renewing of your minds.' In what way are you conformed to this world? How does your mind need renewing? How can you ensure that you imbibe so deeply what God has done, both for you personally and also on the grand scale, that your actions change as a result? Are you willing to 'be transformed' or do you drag your feet?

Pray that God would show you two or three practical ways in which, over the coming week, you can 'present your body as a living sacrifice to God' as a response to his great mercy. Reading Romans will have been worse than useless if we do not change our behaviour as a result.

1 The day is near

Romans 13:8–14

This passage is linked to the previous by the idea of 'owing': we owe taxes, revenue, respect and honour, but what other obligations do Christians have? None, Paul replies, except for love. But, as he then explains, love is the fulfilment of the law: an obligation to love makes other obligations redundant.

This is not just verbal trickery. 'Fulfil the law' does not mean the same as 'obey the law'. The law, in the literal sense of the particularly Jewish framework for life that God gave, has been brought to an end. 'Christ is the end of the law' (10:4): even if 'end' should be translated here as 'goal', it is no longer in operation (once the goal is reached, the journey can end). In Galatians 3:21—4:8, Paul describes the law as a tutor or guardian whose role comes to an end when the child becomes an adult. This, of course, was what the tutor was aiming at all along, but even so the tutor's role is finished. So the law, even the Ten Commandments themselves, are not binding any more: the Christian has no obligations, except to love. By loving our neighbour, we as Christians will be in tune with God's will, and thus will be acting according to the purpose of the law ('fulfilling it'), but we will be doing this in an adult way of working out the implications of love, not in a child's way of obeying commands.

Love as a motivating factor in life is not an alien idea to us, however hard it is to practise. However, Paul also introduces a second factor— the day (of Jesus' return) is near. Verse 12, 'the night is far gone, the day is near', expresses the tension we found in Romans 6—8. Christians should abandon the past (they have died with Christ), but the future is not yet here (they will be raised). In the 'in-between times' we should strive to live 'as in the day' (v. 13), for soon the day will come. Note that there is no new law here, only exhortation.

This lack of laws—moral commands from God which we must obey—is disturbing. Working everything out from the idea of love and the need to 'live honourably as in the day' is difficult: unclear boundaries provide many excuses for immorality. God takes a risk when he treats us as adults, not as children. Do we embrace that, or do we refuse to grow up?

2 The weak and the strong

Romans 14:1–23

In this fascinating chapter, Paul appears to be setting out general principles about relationships within the Christian community, between 'the weak' and 'the strong'. However, the particular issues involved of eating vegetables or meat, or drinking wine (v. 2, 21), clean and unclean (v. 14), and special days (v. 5) all sound like Jewish practices (when Jews could not be sure that meat had been slaughtered correctly, and that meat and wine had not been offered to pagan gods, they avoided both). It seems as if Paul is addressing a particular issue of Jewish Christians and Gentile Christians living together, but without saying this openly. Perhaps this was to make clear the general principles and avoid further polarization.

There are three important points in Paul's argument. The underlying point is actually mentioned last (v. 20): everything is clean, so there is no actual reason for following these particular practices. This fits with the previous passage: particular Jewish practices are no longer binding, but the need to love is. The second point (vv. 3–12) is that judgment is a matter for God, not for us: 'Who are you to pass judgment on servants of another?' (v. 4) and, 'Each of us will be accountable to God' (v. 12).

The third point (vv. 13–23) goes further than the second, for the second point is a bare minimum. We should not condemn our sisters and brothers, but is that really 'loving one another'? Real love goes a step further. Not only should I not despise others for their more restricted practices, but I should be prepared to restrict myself and adopt their practices so as to avoid undermining them. 'The strong' should not merely not despise or condemn 'the weak'; they should be prepared to make sacrifices to help them.

Think about what this would mean in our churches. We often feel that we are doing the right thing by not despising the new music, old hymns, liturgy, old-fashioned approach, impatience, caution, disrespectful dress and behaviour, backward-lookingness, simplicity or confusion of our fellow believers, but for Paul this is merely the first step. Step two, the true Christian way, is to be prepared to adopt their practices if that will help them, and thus to love our neighbour. 'You have the perfect right to do X, but give up that right in order to help others' is a powerful, disturbing doctrine.

3 Imitating Christ

Romans 15:1–13

The climax of Paul's argument from chapter 14 is now reached: 'For Christ did not please himself' (v. 3). This is such a simple statement, but cuts through so many of our arguments. How easily do we argue about our rights, forgetting that our place as one of God's people in the first place is dependent on Jesus giving up everything to save us. Faced with Jesus' example, how can we still try to defend our private concerns? If we were to follow Jesus' example, we would live in harmony with each other (v. 5) to the glory of God (v. 6; cf. also v. 7).

Paul's argument here is further developed in his later letter to the Philippians (2:1–11): 'Let each of you look not to your own interests, but to the interests of others. Let the same mind be in you that was in Christ Jesus, who... emptied himself... humbled himself... so that... every tongue should confess that Jesus Christ is Lord, to the glory of God the Father.' Thus, Paul's ethics are the same whichever way one looks at them. Imitating Christ produces the same result as following love, both of which are the same as presenting our bodies as living sacrifices to God and living honourably, as in the day (which is near), which Paul himself described as 'putting on the Lord Jesus Christ' (13:14). However you look at it, we have moved from Adam to Christ and should live accordingly.

In verses 7–13, Paul's discussion of 'the weak' and 'the strong' gives way to the old Jew/Gentile distinctions. These verses form a conclusion in many ways to the formal part of the letter; from verse 14 onwards, Paul speaks more personally about himself and greets people by name. Here we see that all of Paul's discussion of Jew and Gentile earlier in Romans was not just a theological exercise. Theology should be practical: now we see that Paul had the practical difficulties of getting Jewish and Gentile followers of Jesus to 'welcome one another' in mind all the time. His summary in verses 8–9 is carefully chosen. The same Jesus is the servant of both Jews and Gentiles; it is not that Jesus is only good for Gentiles. For Jews, Jesus' effect is to 'confirm the promises given to the patriarchs'. Jesus does not overthrow the Old Testament promises (3:31), the word of God has not failed (9:6), and God's call is irrevocable (11:29). The expansion of God's purpose to involve Gentiles is purely the result of God's amazing mercy, but the expansion has happened and should result in rejoicing. Indeed, the Old Testament itself confirms this (vv. 9–12).

4 Paul's plans

Romans 15:14–33

Suddenly the tone of the letter changes. Paul is no longer proclaiming the truth and urging his readers to Christ-like behaviour, but becomes polite and almost apologetic. Many scholars see hidden in today's reading the real reason for Romans being written in the first place, or at least the reason it has the shape it has.

In verses 14–24, Paul seems keen to explain his past actions and his decision to come to Rome. In this he highlights his particular role, given to him by God (v. 16; cf. Galatians 1:16) of ministering to the Gentiles. Two aspects of this are noteworthy. First, he talks of 'the offering of the Gentiles', with Paul performing a 'priestly service' (the only time in the New Testament that the idea of a Christian priest is found). This rather strange way of describing evangelism among Gentiles is probably deliberately echoing the later parts of Isaiah (66:20 in particular) in order to emphasize that this incoming of Gentiles is in accordance with the Old Testament. Second, he describes his aim as winning 'obedience from the Gentiles' (v. 18 cf. 1:5). This is again a somewhat unusual phrase. Presumably, it was chosen to emphasize that the incoming Gentiles are not immoral; Paul's gospel might be 'law-free' but it is not 'lawless'.

Then, in verses 25–33, Paul mentions his forthcoming trip to Jerusalem, carrying money that his churches in Europe have given for the Christians in Jerusalem (see 1 Corinthians 16:1–4). The idea of one group of Christians giving to poor Christians elsewhere seems unremarkable, if admirable. However, Paul sees it in terms of Jews and Gentiles: this is the Gentile Christians 'paying back' the Jewish Christians for their spiritual blessings, the branches contributing to the natural tree at the same time as drawing on its roots (11:17–24). More significantly, however, the giving and receiving of this support would, in effect, be the recognition that both Jewish and Gentile Christians form 'one body', within which there is naturally a sharing of resources. This is why Paul is unsure whether the gift will be accepted (vv. 30–32): those on the receiving end know just as clearly what accepting it would mean. Throughout Romans, Paul has been arguing for a Christian gospel that embraces both Jews and Gentiles, bringing them into one people of God. What will happen in Jerusalem will reveal whether, on the larger scale, he has persuaded others of this. It is in the giving and receiving of help, encouragement and gifts that many of our underlying beliefs are revealed.

5 Greetings

Romans 16:1–16

What are your feelings as you read this long list of greetings? Here we cannot avoid feeling that we are reading someone else's letter, which of course is exactly what we have been doing all along. This great theological masterpiece is, in fact, a letter written in a particular context, to particular people whom we do not know. God is at work through the everyday and particular in our lives, not just in some abstract or universal way.

The fact that there are so many greetings has intrigued scholars. Paul has never been to Rome (1:13; 15:22), so how can he know so many people there? Perhaps this is the wrong question: it is not surprising that Paul had met a number of people over the years who were now in Rome. What is interesting is that he chose to greet them all by name in his letter, when presumably many of them were not his closest friends. Here we again get the sense of Paul's care and sensitivity in his approach to the church in Rome. Paul is keen to build bridges with the church there, and what better way is there for doing this than by highlighting his personal contact with many people there? These greetings would generate a feeling that the church in Rome is already united with Paul through so many common links.

These greetings also provide something of a snapshot of ministry within the early Christian communities. Important within it is the place of women. Paul begins by commending to the church Phoebe, who has been a 'benefactor' of Paul and of others, and is called a 'deacon' of the church. Whether 'deacon' is quite the right translation here is unclear, for the word itself can just mean 'servant', but soon enough the church was using it to describe those holding a particular office (e.g. Philippians 1:1; 1 Timothy 3:8–13). Prisca and Aquila (mentioned with a Roman connection in Acts 18:1–2) seem to have been important figures, not only for Paul but for 'all the churches of the Gentiles' (v. 4). It is intriguing that Prisca, the woman, is mentioned first. We also read of Andronicus and Julia who are 'prominent among the apostles', which certainly seems a lofty description.

We often think that our modern age, with its advanced communications, is the age of 'networks'. This list of greetings may make us think again. Are our churches interconnected, sharing gifts with each other, or are they isolated fortresses?

6 Final summary

Romans 16:17–27

As Paul's longest and historically most significant letter draws to a close, we find two closing exhortations or blessings separated by a handful of greetings (vv. 21–23). Both reflect the main thrust of the letter and are, in a sense, summaries. This fits with the common practice of the time of giving a closing summary or conclusion to a letter (see, for example, 1 Corinthians 16:22; Galatians 6:11–16). These summaries can point us to what Paul thought was the 'main point' of his letter. Here, the first (vv. 17–20) concentrates on the practical, the second (vv. 25–27) on the theological, but as always the two are closely related.

The first summary (vv. 17–20) is an attack on those who cause dissensions and who cause offence. We are immediately reminded of chapter 14 and 'the weak' and 'the strong'. There, we noted that while Paul approaches the issue in general terms, it looked as if it was a practical outworking of the Jew/Gentile issue. Those who make this into a divisive issue are deceivers (v. 18). They are closer to Satan than Jesus, for God is a God of peace, not division (v. 20).

The second summary (vv. 25–27) emphasizes that Paul's gospel (remember how obsessed with it he seemed in 1:1–16?) is not a novelty. Yes, it has been revealed only recently, but it has been God's plan 'for long ages' (v. 25) and was witnessed to by the prophets (v. 26). This message is for the Gentiles, but again Paul emphasizes that it is 'according to the command of the eternal God'—it is not some novelty dreamt up by Paul—and it brings about 'obedience of faith' (v. 26; cf. 1:5; 15:18): the Gentiles become moral, pious followers of God. Paul's espousal of 'faith not law' does not undermine obedience.

Right until the end, Paul continues to defend the right of Gentile Christians to be part of the people of God, to urge that Jew and Gentile Christians live together in peace, and to point out the continuity between his message and the Old Testament. His concern to establish equality within the Church, and to explain God's consistency and purpose, are an example to be pondered.

Guidelines

The theological exposition and unveiling of God's plan within Romans is important. It is striking, however, that in the end it comes down to Christians being urged to accept one another—indeed, to go out of our way to help the other (ch. 14)—for in doing so we will be following the example of Jesus (15:1, 7). This acceptance and help should be expressed in practical ways (15:25–30), networking together Christians in different places as well as from different backgrounds (16:1–16). The Christians form 'one body', whether we think of that locally (12:3–8) or internationally (15:29–33). Dissension is to be avoided, for it does not serve Christ (16:18). This overall meaning is similar to John 13:35: 'By this everyone will know that you are my disciples, if you have love for one another.'

The message is simple; doing it is difficult. Are there ways in which you can commit yourself, with God's help, to building trust and mutuality among Christians of different 'types'? Paul's letter to the Romans tells us that this is a goal well worth pursuing.

LAMENTATIONS

The book of Lamentations is a collection of five poems that mark the response to the singularly defining event in the history of ancient Israel—the fall of Jerusalem, the destruction of the temple and the deportation of the citizenry of Jerusalem to Babylon—which took place in 587BC. The five short poems of Lamentations attest to very human responses to the destruction of Jerusalem and the cessation of its political, religious and social structures.

A variety of responses to disaster are recorded in Lamentations, without any recognizable order. They represent a literary grieving process in which the cacophony of images and feelings provides a sense of the chaos experienced by the community. In spite of the seeming dis-organization, the poet provides a sense of order through the use of an alphabetic acrostic. In the first four chapters, each verse follows the sequence of the letters of the Hebrew alphabet, and the number of verses in the fifth poem corresponds to the number of consonants in the Hebrew alphabet. The use of the acrostic provides a sense that, in spite of the fact that the violence recounted in the collection is on the verge of being overwhelming, it is contained.

Distinctively, Lamentations looks neither to the history of Israel nor to its future, but attests the very human need to give voice to the pain of loss and suffering. In so doing, the poems attest the perspective of the survivors, who survey the ruins of their lives and call out from the depths of despair to God. Through prayer, the community expresses its dismay and distress. Even more importantly, the people grapple with questions that resonate within the modern context. They wonder about God's provision and character in the light of such terrible events and such depth of suffering.

The poems continue to be read in the Jewish synagogue on the 9th of Ab to commemorate the destruction of Jerusalem and the temple in 587BC by the Babylonians and in AD70 by the Romans. Many Christian communities use its liturgy during the Lenten season. This week's worth of readings is designed to provide an entry into this remarkable poetry and to introduce some of the ways a community grappled with crisis.

The biblical references correspond to the NRSV.

1 The power and possibility of reminiscence

Lamentations 1:1–12

The poems of Lamentations depict the disaster that befell the community through a series of different speaking voices. In the beginning of the first chapter, we are introduced to the first one—an eyewitness narrator—who speaks again in 2:1–19 and perhaps in chapter 4. The role of this impersonal reporter is to recount the destruction that has occurred and to relate the ongoing suffering of the inhabitants of the city.

Rather than simply providing a calm report of the disaster, the eyewitness conveys the more human aspect of the tragedy by a variety of methods. In the first place, he speaks through the form of a dirge, the type of elegy one might use at a funeral. He mourns the loss of the city as if it were a deceased loved one. Through another means, he evokes a sense of empathy and pathos not expected from a reporter. The narrator personifies the city of Jerusalem as a woman who has suffered a multitude of calamities. It was natural to depict cities as feminine because, in Hebrew, 'city' has a feminine grammatical form. Elsewhere in the prophetic literature, cities are personified as women who receive oracles of judgment and salvation (Isaiah 47 and 60—62; Ezekiel 16 and 23). In Lamentations, Lady Jerusalem is like a widow, a woman who has been spurned by her paramours, and a mother who has lost her children. The destruction of the gates of the city, its buildings and its temple figured as a woman in pain heightens the sense of distress and drives home a sense of loss, confusion, disorientation and despair. In fact, every time some disaster is recounted it is spoken of in relation to Lady Jerusalem—'her gates', 'her citizens' and so on.

Although the image of the personified city finds its closest parallel in Mesopotamian lament literature, where the goddess of a city mourns the destruction of her capital and its temple, and the suffering of its inhabitants, in Lamentations the city itself weeps as a woman in travail. The poet figures her in great distress, holding her middle as her head bows down from shame, with tears sliding down her cheeks to alight in the dust beneath her feet. Finally, the narrator drives home with bitter honesty the plight of the city when he repeatedly says that 'there is no one to comfort her'. Unlike Job, whose three friends came to comfort him in a type of mourning ceremony (Job 2:11–13), Lady Jerusalem sits alone (1:1) and without comfort. The lack of someone to supply this role highlights the enormity of her situation. This is mourning without end, without even a hope of its completion.

Lamentations begins with the heart-wrenching details of tragedy and human pain beyond measure. Even in the midst of ongoing suffering, the poet delineates the distress, he calls it to mind and mourns it in religious language. In the light of no human comforter, he brings to mind and to voice the details of the tragedy, to call forth a divine comforter. His actions signify one significant means of coping with tragedy—remembering it and recalling it.

2 'Rage, rage against the dying of the light'
Lamentations 1:12–22; 2:18–22

The eyewitness reporter in the first half of chapter 1 spoke of Jerusalem in language reminiscent of a funeral. As if in protest against the poet's depiction of her as a deceased loved one, Lady Jerusalem speaks emphatically. Already she had interrupted the rote report of the narrator at the end of 1:9 and 11, but from verse 12 to the end of the chapter Lady Jerusalem calls to onlookers and passers-by—indeed, to the audience—to bear witness to her suffering. In so doing, she reiterates themes already mentioned by the eyewitness, but conveys them through her own perspective. While weeping on account of her suffering and that experienced by the inhabitants of the city—those whom she calls her children (1:16)—she claims that there is no one to comfort her (1:16–17).

Lady Jerusalem portrays herself as the recipient of punishment instigated and carried out by God, depicted as the divine warrior, and his human agents—enemy nations. In addition, she acknowledges responsibility for her fate in a confession of sin (1:14, 18, 20). In the ancient world, suffering on this scale was conceived of as punishment for sin. Nevertheless, Lady Jerusalem's speech accentuates the unimaginable human scale of the suffering. In some respects, the portrayal of the human toll of the disaster overshadows the recognition that the people are culpable for their fate. The emphasis suggests that the people recognized that the repercussions for covenant disobedience far outweighed the crime. By bringing this to the attention of God, they hope for an overturning of the present distress and for renewal.

The voice of Lady Jerusalem appears to fade at the end of chapter 1, for she no longer interrupts the narrator, who speaks again of the tragedy in 2:1–19. However, the narrator, moved by her distress and by the fate of her children, urges her to cry out (2:18–19). The eyewitness encourages Lady Jerusalem to cry aloud, to let tears fall daily and nightly, and to pour out her heart to the Lord. Only after his insistence does Lady Jerusalem speak again. In the hope of alleviation of her distress, she closes by recalling the suffering of unaccountable victims and the role that her foes played in its accomplishment (2:20–22).

The emphasis in these passages is on the need to articulate suffering. The alleviation of this kind of suffering can only come about through divine intervention. For the people struggling in post-war Judah, one coping mechanism was through the articulation of pain to the deity, in the hope that God would intervene in a restorative way.

3 Hope in the midst of despair

Lamentations 3:1–39

Although Lady Jerusalem's voice fades, perhaps in response to the level of her grief, a third speaking voice picks up her lament. The third poem begins with 'I am the man who has seen affliction' (v. 1, NIV). This is the single suffering male figure—a strong man reduced to vocalizing an individual lament that utilizes language reminiscent of physical abuse. His voice is a counterbalance to that of Lady Jerusalem. Although there have been attempts to identify the speaker with either the prophet Jeremiah (to whom the book is traditionally attributed), or one of the kings of the now defunct state, or with an 'everyman', the figure of the third chapter might represent the experience of the exiles, as A. Berlin suggests. Their experience would form a nice counterbalance to that of the city of Jerusalem and the population that remained in Judah.

The man begins with the suffering he has experienced (vv. 1–18). Like

Lady Jerusalem, he too has seen affliction and been subject to divine wrath. His focus is less on the disaster in the city of Jerusalem and more on his own experience. He complains of physical distress, abandonment, isolation and the attack of wild animals, who probably represent, figuratively, the enemies. It is only in verse 18 that he acknowledges and names God as the ultimate source of his affliction. More traumatic still is that he feels completely abandoned by God (vv. 17–18).

In spite of his seemingly ignoble fate, from within his wall of pain the individual sufferer issues forth with one of the most beautiful litanies on the mercy and love of God in all of scripture (vv. 19–24). His reflection on the nature of the deity to have constant love and compassion falls at the very centre of the poem and indeed at the heart of the collection as a whole. It attests to a fundamental belief that God's rule is defined by compassion and justice, which will be actualized in the human realm. Furthermore, it asserts a profound expectation that God will intervene to bring salvation. After his hopeful interlude, the man reflects on how he came to such a perception with words akin to the wisdom traditions of ancient Israel (vv. 25–39). In his view, misfortune and blessing stem from God. Because he understands that suffering is redemptive, he advocates silent submission and patient expectation. His belief that good and ill come from God, that suffering should be borne with confidence, and that God will restore health and well-being represents a didactic message akin to the view espoused by Job's friends. In the midst of tragedy, the suffering individual finds hope in his belief in God's goodness and sovereignty.

Unlike the eyewitness and Lady Jerusalem, who insist on shouting out experiences of disaster, the suffering individual of chapter 3 advocates silent submission in the face of tragedy. His belief represents another way to respond to crisis and tragedy: accept one's lot and hope for divine renewal and recompense.

4 Penitential prayer

Lamentations 3:40–66

For the first time in the book, a communal speaking voice ('we') raises a prayer to the deity. Through this communal lament, the people examine their ways and repent of their sins, expecting the return of God's protection and provision. Again, there is a declaration of the cultural belief that sin evokes divine anger and punishment. In response, the people express their repentance in prayer. The role that sin has played is acknowledged elsewhere in 1:5, 8, 18; 2:14; 4:6, 13; 5:7 and 16, but the passage in chapter 3 actually shows the people at prayer with their hands outstretched.

Here, in response to the claims of the individual sufferer about the magnitude of God's mercy, the people pray expecting to be forgiven and for a new future. In verse 42, however, faced with the acute reality of their ongoing hardship, the people accuse God of failing to forgive them. While not rejecting the power of repentance, the lament acknowledges that God has turned away from their prayer. Their prayer cannot reach divine ears because God has enveloped himself in a cloud (v. 44). Elsewhere in the Old Testament, as in the story of the exodus, the cloud is the location through which divine presence and protection are mediated (Exodus 13:21–22; 14:19–24; 40:34–38). Here, it distinctively marks divine absence. In the face of tragedy, the community wonders where is their God. They resume their complaint in the hope that God will hear them.

An individual sufferer responds to the complaint of the people (vv. 48–66). Although he reiterates examples of his own physical suffering, the speech of the lone figure reveals a remarkable transition. Within his recital, the individual envisions God as an ally. Although pursued and harassed by enemies, he claims that God will fight for him. The individual responds to the petitioners with an alternative vision. He perceives God's willingness to fight on behalf of his covenant people, in spite of what appears to be his unwillingness to do so. One needs only to continue to affirm the righteous dealings of God.

The communal lament and the lament of the individual show the two different responses to ongoing suffering encountered already in the poems of the collection. On the one hand, there is the need to present the painful current situation. On the other hand, there is the assertion of God's intentions of goodwill and justice. The two are held in tension as the hopeful vision is eclipsed by tragedy.

5 Divine suffering on a human scale

Lamentations 4:1–22

The fourth chapter contains a lengthy and sustained focus on the human toll of the catastrophe. In verses 1–20, the reporter recounts the reversal that has occurred. Everything that was once good is now in a terrible state.

Verse 1 takes two apparently enduring materials—gold and stone—and suggests the great contrast between their conditions before and after the disaster. The second verse clarifies the imagery of the first. The children of Jerusalem are metaphorically related to the gold and to the vessels of a potter. In addition to the ruins of the city lie the ruins of the people who experienced the tragedy. In this poem, the catastrophe is related to every member of society in horrific detail: children, elders, maidens, mothers, princes and men have all experienced disaster. The fourth chapter, then, resumes the violent images that were found at the end of chapter 3. Through this, the message of hope found at the very centre of the book, almost as its theological nub, gives way to the tragedy that eclipses it. No longer is the focus on the city itself. Here, the suffering of the inhabitants takes pride of place.

The community interjects its first personal plural 'we' voice in the midst of the litany on human suffering in verses 17–20. These verses represent the most pessimistic outlook in the entire collection. There is no hope. In spite of the fact that the people look vainly for some positive sign, there is none. A different and more positive future remains at bay because even the king has been deported.

Like the other poems, and particularly aligned with chapters 1 and 2, the fourth chapter portrays the divine agency behind the distress. The fact that the intensity of the pain is presented as the result of divine intention suggests that only through divine intervention can it be alleviated. The poem closes by linking the fate of Judah with the fate of the nations. The poet confidently predicts to Edom—one of the foreign nations who participated in the destruction of Jerusalem—that God will requite the enemies of Judah. Through their defeat, Judah will be restored. During the exile, the intertwining fates of Judah and foreign nations became clearer, such that the exaltation of Jerusalem would come about along with the defeat of the other nations. In spite of evidence to the contrary, especially when considering the sorry state of the victims, the poet predicts that the future restoration of Jerusalem is nigh.

6 Divine sovereignty

Lamentations 5:1–22

In the fifth poem of Lamentations, the communal voice ('we') once again rises to the fore. All of the speaking voices previously encountered join together in the final chapter. As the lament of the people, it forms a fitting conclusion to the collection as a whole. The community laments its circumstances in a lengthy litany of despair, which captures again the various aspects of the tragedy (vv. 1–18). Just as in the rest of the book, however, the confession of trust or vote of confidence in the Lord in verse 19 is eclipsed again by uncertainty (vv. 20–22).

The first part of the lament has a sustained concentration on the dire present. It is a tragic vision recalling famine, violence and the severity of imperial taxation. As a summary, the people hauntingly sigh, 'The joy of our hearts has ceased; our dancing has been turned to mourning' (v. 15).

The community finds solace or strength in their understanding of the nature and character of God. They affirm their belief in the eternal and everlasting kingship of the deity in verse 19. In spite of their confidence in divine rule, there remains a question over whether or not God will choose to be their king. The communal lament fittingly ends the collection.

We have seen heretofore that the people are experiencing ongoing suffering of such magnitude that it could be conceived of as human suffering on a divine scale, but throughout the poems of Lamentations the constant depiction of God as an enemy or aggressor, who even chooses enemy nations to act as agents of his wrath, conveys the belief that God is ultimately in control of events, however terrible they might be. Confidence in God's sovereignty is, therefore, never questioned in the collection. The concern rests on whether or not God will choose to be in a covenant relationship with this despairing people again. Hence, the collection ends on a note of concern, a painful query regarding the intentions of the deity. Will he, in fact, choose to reject this people for ever, to allow his anger to hold sway?

Lamentations uses language of disaster found in the literature of neighbouring countries in the ancient Near East. Although the Mesopotamian laments that commemorated the destruction of cities may have influenced the themes encountered in the biblical book of Lamentations, there is one crucial difference. The Mesopotamian laments conclude with a happy ending, in which the deity returns and the city and temple are restored. There is no positive conclusion to Lamentations because suffering continues. Even more tragic still, the divine comforter so often sought in the collection fails to return. The community is left on the precipice of tragedy, wondering about the renewal of divine presence and protection.

Guidelines

The poems of Lamentations are not easy to read, as they are primarily concerned with the recollection of tragedy. They witness to the cacophony of human emotions that accompany disaster—despair, anger, hopelessness and dismay. However, their placement in the canon and within the liturgy of churches and synagogues attests to the fact that they remain appropriate for today's people of faith. Questions about the scope of human suffering in the light of God's justice, mercy and love are raised constantly by individuals who suffer situations of distress and communities that face war, starvation and disease. Lamentations provides an example of a faithful response to crisis without giving any easy answers.

Sadly, the one voice most desperately sought in the book remains silent. God never answers the laments of the people as he does in the book of Job. Because the people believe that the physical circumstances around them attest to God's presence and providence, they continue to mourn the absence of their God. Like Lady Jerusalem, who had no comforter, they have no divine comforter. Nevertheless, reality does not occasion abject and silent acceptance, but penitence and protest.

It is important to note that in spite of the fact that hope and pain are held in tension throughout the poems, and even though confidence is eclipsed by tragedy, the people prayed. Each poem of the book is written in the language of liturgy, including elements consistent with the dirge, the individual and communal lament and the confession of sin. Although seemingly sorrowful, the prayers of Lamentations are ultimately hopeful because, through these agonizing prayers, a war-torn and war-weary people fundamentally expressed their belief in the sovereignty of their God. They prayed ultimately because they believed that God would hear their prayers. Whether that God would choose to intervene was a different and more tragic story, but the belief that God would at least hear them underlies each line of their painful prayers.

FURTHER READING:

A. Berlin, *Lamentations*, Old Testament Library, Westminster/John Knox, 2002.

F.W. Dobbs-Allsopp, *Lamentations*, Interpretation, John Knox Press, 2002.

I. Provan, *Lamentations*, New Century Bible, Marshall Pickering, 1991.

JESUS IS KING

The diminishing importance of monarchy in our world has made 'king' a less than obvious model with which to understand the significance of Jesus. The persistence of its use, however, within both older hymns and modern songs, reflects its prominence within the biblical material. 'Jesus as king' does not only operate on an explicit level through much of the New Testament; there is increasing recognition of its importance as a 'given' in texts where its profile is less obvious. The kingship of Jesus particularly dominates the Passion narrative of Mark's Gospel, which we will follow through Holy Week, and in Easter week we will look at the 'royal' understanding that the early Church gave to his resurrection. Engaging with these passages not only deepens our understanding of the significance of Jesus' death and resurrection but also provides exciting implications for our faith today.

These notes use the New Revised Standard Version (NRSV).

1 The agony of the king

Mark 14:32–42

The ancient world certainly knew how to make heroes out of its kings and leaders. Whether it was expressed in the legends of Achilles and Hector or through recalling later, more historical figures, such as Leonidas of Sparta, the image of a king going bravely and calmly to his death was one that many people found immensely attractive and inspiring. Followers of Judaism were no exception. At the time of Jesus, young children were still being raised on stories of the Maccabean martyrs going staunchly to their deaths for a cause they believed in.

Mark's account of Gethsemane may be deliberately intended to contrast with this imagery. John's Gospel may show a serene Jesus exercising full control over the events that led to his death but here in Mark's account the emphasis is upon his horror and anguish at what awaited him over the next few hours. Jesus is 'distressed and agitated'

(v. 33), he is 'deeply grieved' (v. 34), and every single detail seems to point to the agonizing struggle between what he wanted and the will of his Father. The contrast with 'heroic kingship' could hardly be fuller.

It is through his vivid portrayal of this painful and very human struggle, however, that Mark presents his deepest insight into what it really meant for Jesus to be the Son of God. Whatever its later associations, Son of God was a title previously used of Israel (Hosea 11:1) and its kings (Psalm 2:7). It held out the ideal of an intimacy grounded in struggling obedience, but the history of both the nation and its leaders showed the persistent failure of this ideal to become a reality. It is here in Gethsemane that Jesus uses the intimate term 'Abba' to address his Father (v. 36), making Mark's point that it is Jesus' human struggle to obey God's will that truly defines his Sonship.

The role of the disciples in this episode is to serve as a contrast. Like Israel and all its previous kings, the disciples fail in their vocation to 'keep awake and pray' (v. 38). The theme of discipleship is never far beneath the surface of Mark's account, and this is a summons for us to enter into the same struggle of faithful obedience. Above all, however, it is an episode that speaks of the uniqueness of Jesus—Jesus the perfect and unique Son through and because of his perfect and unique obedience to the will of God.

2 The arrest of the king

Mark 14:43–52

Yesterday's reading emphasized the correlation between the uniqueness of Jesus' obedience and the uniqueness of his status as the Son of God. This theme is developed further in Mark's account of his arrest, where he shows how Jesus stood completely alone against his enemies. Judas leads an armed crowd against him sent by the 'triple alliance' of the chief priests, the scribes and the elders (v. 43). Not only have the leaders of various strands of Judaism therefore turned against him, but even one of his own strand, 'one of the Twelve', has chosen to desert and betray him. Jesus' vocation is one that he has to face completely alone.

The account that follows shows why this has to be the case. By revealing the one to arrest with the 'sign' of a kiss (v. 45), Judas

unwittingly reveals the act of love lying at the heart of Jesus' submission. This revelation, however, is completely lost on Jesus' last
remaining supporters, as one of them draws a sword and attacks the
high priest's slave (v. 47). Jesus' response shows how all those bearing
'swords and clubs' around him have totally misunderstood his kingship. He isn't a brigand or rebel using force to bring about his aims but
someone called to make himself completely open to arrest, knowing
that this and his subsequent death would bring to fulfilment God's
plans in the scriptures (vv. 48–49).

Mark underlines the uniqueness of this calling by showing how the
solitariness of Jesus became total at this point: 'All of them deserted him
and fled' (v. 50). The condition of all those around him is such that
Jesus has to be completely alone as the forces of evil come against him.
This is drawn out by Mark's unique account of the young man who
'was following' Jesus. He too flees from Jesus, and his nakedness in the
garden reminds us of Adam and Eve and the plight of all humanity
through its disobedience to God (vv. 51–52). What Jesus had to do
he had to do alone, because even comprehending the nature of his
kingship was completely beyond the rest of humanity.

3 The king before the council

Mark 14:53–65

As Jesus is taken before the Sanhedrin, Mark's emphasis upon the
totality of the opposition leads into an equally heavy stress upon its
venom. The entire council are determined to bring about Jesus' death,
and they are prepared to use whatever means they can (v. 55). However,
three times between verses 55 and 59 we see these efforts thwarted as
the council are unable to find true testimony and those who give false
testimony are unable to agree. The silence of Jesus shows that none of
their accusations needs to be answered and the mounting frustration of
the high priest (v. 60) reflects the deeper frustration and anger of the
powers of evil in their determination to consume him.

It is in the middle of all this anger and darkness that Mark once again
chooses to reveal more of the nature of Jesus' kingship. Keen to push
things to a conclusion, the high priest speaks once again, this time

asking, 'Are you the Messiah/Christ, the Son of the Blessed One?' Jesus affirms that he is, but the crucial part is what follows as he expresses his understanding of what this actually means. As he has done throughout the Gospel, Jesus draws upon the title of Son of Man to speak about himself, but this time he quotes from its original context in Daniel 7:13 (v. 62). 'Son of Man' was a term that Daniel used to refer to the righteous Israelites who were called to endure terrible suffering from 'the beasts' before one day receiving complete vindication and glory from God. In using this term in conjunction with Daniel's unmistakable imagery, Jesus is making a very precise claim about his self-understanding. Alone before his enemies and ready to undergo appalling suffering, Jesus is the one who will fulfil the calling to righteous suffering that Israel had been unable to live up to. He confirms that he is Israel's messianic king and, as he does so, affirms his understanding of what that kingship means. As Israel's king, he is her representative, called to assume her vocation of suffering in order to deal with evil.

Once again, the nature of our Christian discipleship is more than hinted at. The reference to being 'seated at the right hand of the Power' (v. 62) recalls Jesus' earlier statement that such positions in his kingdom would come from following a similar path of servanthood (10:35–45). The main emphasis here, however, is upon the king, not the subjects. Living up to Israel's vocation can come only through being under the representative king, who fulfils it so fully.

4 The king before the governor

Mark 15:1–20

It's as the Jewish leaders hand him over to the Roman governor that the theme of Jesus' kingship becomes fully explicit. 'Are you the King of the Jews?' is Pilate's blunt question (v. 2). With the oblique reply, 'You say so', Jesus affirms that this is true, but the rest of the passage—indeed the rest of the book—shows that it is a kingship totally different from what Pilate either meant or understood.

To unpack this further, Mark introduces Barabbas, who is exactly the sort of figure that Pilate would have understood. Standing in the tradition of the Maccabees, Barabbas symbolizes the type of 'king' that

Israel was increasingly looking for in the years that preceded the Jewish revolt. He was a rebel and in prison alongside others who saw murder and uprising as their nation's only option (v. 7). Offered the release of 'the King of the Jews', the crowd opt instead for this 'false king' (v. 11). Jesus is taken away to be crucified (v. 15) and Israel continues on the path that leads to the ultimate destruction in AD70.

The details that follow speak with terrible irony of the king whom Israel has rejected. Led into the palace, a 'coronation' takes place as the soldiers dress Jesus in a purple robe and place a crown of thorns on his head (vv. 16–17). Full of mockery, they salute Jesus and kneel in homage to him (vv. 18–19), completely unaware of the truth they are indicating. Israel's calling was to an innocent suffering that would bring the Gentiles to worship the true God. The nation may have rejected this calling but it is being fulfilled here through the representative they have also rejected—Jesus, 'the King of the Jews'.

5 The crucifixion of the king

Mark 15:25–39

As Jesus is executed, so the mockery continues. People passing by and even the others being crucified join with the Jewish leaders in heaping insults upon him (vv. 29–32). This mockery continues to focus on the claim to kingship that is described in the charge against him (v. 26). 'He saved others; he cannot save himself,' the leaders declare. 'Let the Messiah, the King of Israel, come down from the cross now, so that we may see and believe' (v. 32).

The irony here lies within the fact that it is Jesus' very kingship that compels him to stay on the cross. As the whole of Israel seems to reject him, so he as its king shares the consequences of the path that they have chosen, being executed between two Barabbas-like bandits (v. 27). Darkness comes down and at three o'clock Jesus cries out, 'My God, my God, why have you forsaken me?' (v. 34). Rejected by everyone and abandoned even by God, Jesus is now completely alone. With one last piece of mockery and misunderstanding from an onlooker, he gives a loud cry and dies (vv. 36–37).

It's a bleak picture, full of almost complete darkness. But as Jesus dies, alone and in horrific agony, the mystery is intensified by two remarkable events. The mockery he received for predicting the temple's destruction takes an ironic twist as its curtain is torn from top to bottom (v. 38). Somehow, in some way, the death of Israel's king has made the temple obsolete. And meanwhile, back at the cross, a Gentile centurion, who has heard Jesus' cry of dereliction and seen the manner of his death, somehow makes the startling equation that Mark has been driving at all along. It is through, not despite, these events that Jesus is shown to be a man who is truly the Son of God (v. 39).

What does Mark mean by all this? He means that although Israel chose to go another way, its unacknowledged king went with them, sharing in their suffering and abandonment. And as he did this, so Jesus became perfect through obedience, somehow fulfilling the calling of Israel to be the Servant, the Son of Man and the Son of God. This suffering obedience of 'the King of the Jews' somehow opened a door for the Gentiles to see God and somehow provides acceptance and forgiveness for all who accept his reign.

6 The burial of a much-loved king

Mark 15:40–47

Some of the more pressing questions posed to orthodox Christianity in recent years have been raised by feminists. Can a male Jesus who calls God 'Father' and is known as Son of Man and Son of God ever be acceptable to women? Understanding Jesus as king might seem most problematic of all, since it appears to promote the subservience of women to yet another male authority.

Without answering all of these questions, Mark's account of what happened after the death of Jesus offers us some help. His theological emphasis has been on the solitary nature of Jesus' death but now we learn that a significant group of his female followers have remained faithful (v. 40). It's important to appreciate the radical nature of the details that Mark records. For a travelling rabbi to have women disciples was unheard of at this time, and the fact that these women 'provided for him' (v. 41) shows that their relationship with Jesus was one of enrichment and empowerment. The greatest testimony to this radical inclusivity is the devotion that continued in Mary Magdalene, Mary and Salome, long after Jesus' male disciples had all run away.

It was society that denied recognition to these women, and this is reflected in the fact that only a well-placed man is able to approach Pilate to gain Jesus' body. Joseph of Arimathea is described as 'a respected member of the council' (Luke tells us he didn't consent to Jesus' death) and his wealth and position allow him to provide Jesus with an expensive tomb (v. 46). It is with definite approval that Mark tells us that Joseph was 'waiting expectantly for the kingdom of God' (v. 43) but the statement opens up a possible contrast with the women. The reason for the unstinting devotion of Mary Magdalene, Mary, Salome and the other women was because they had *already* experienced God's kingship through their relationship with Jesus. In a world where they were second-class citizens, these women had encountered a king who gave them affirmation and the full opportunity to flourish. But this Jesus was now dead. All those dreams of emancipation and empowerment were shattered. Evil appeared to be back in charge of a cruel world, without hope. They were in for a surprise…

Guidelines

Easter day is for celebrating the resurrection of Jesus and his status as the risen king. However, this is possible only because of the lonely, tortured and rejected figure that we have looked at over the last few days. As our thoughts turn to the significance of Jesus' resurrection, take some time to reflect upon an ancient summary of how these two images relate and their implications for us as we seek to follow this king.

Let the same mind be in you that was in [King] Jesus, who, though he was in the form of God, did not regard equality with God as something to be exploited, but emptied himself, taking the form of a slave, being born in human likeness. And being found in human form, he humbled himself and became obedient to the point of death—even death on a cross. Therefore God also highly exalted him and gave him the name that is above every name, so that at the name of Jesus every knee should bend, in heaven and on earth and under the earth, and every tongue should confess that [King] Jesus is Lord, to the glory of God the Father. (Philippians 2:5–11)

1 An empty tomb and a startling claim

Mark 16:1–8

The Sabbath has ended and the devotion of the women to the memory of their king continues as they make their way to Jesus' tomb to anoint his body. Mark's emphasis upon the persistence of their devotion combines with an awareness of the return of their vulnerability and lack of empowerment. Joseph of Arimathea had sealed the tomb (15:46) but he is not present. The women had been able to minister to Jesus in Galilee (15:41), but now even their opportunity to care for his body is threatened by the return of their dependent and secondary status: 'Who will roll away the stone *for us* from the entrance to the tomb?' (v. 3).

A dramatic surprise confronts the women, as they find that the large stone is no longer blocking their way (v. 4). This sight takes on a symbolic significance as they enter the tomb to receive the news that overturns all their assumptions about reality. A young man informs them that their crucified master is no longer there because he is no longer dead. The man shows them the empty space where the body had been laid and makes the astonishing claim that Jesus has been raised (vv. 5–6). It is little wonder that the women are alarmed. They are being confronted by the claim that the story of their relationship with Jesus and everything he gave them is not over. He has been raised and is awaiting the resumption of their relationship in Galilee. This sudden challenge to their perception of reality is reflected in an immediate act of empowerment. Courts of law at that time may have required the evidence of two male witnesses, but the rule of their king is different. It is these disenfranchised and oppressed women who are called to be the first witnesses of the event that changed everything about the world they lived in (v. 7).

It is here that Mark's Gospel suddenly and very abruptly ends. Its final verse reports that the women fled, full of terror and amazement, and said nothing to anyone because they were afraid (v. 8). Given the predictions of Jesus' resurrection throughout the Gospel (8:31; 9:31; 10:34) and the details of verse 7, the strongest probability is that

Mark's original ending has been lost. As it stands, however, the uncertainty of Mark's ending does provide a challenge. The women are terrified because they have been presented with a claim that, if true, will change everything—but it also entails a response. Are they, and we, prepared to believe that the king is alive, and are we prepared to set out to meet him?

2 Called to proclaim the risen king and his rule
Matthew 28:16–20

With Mark including no account of a resurrection appearance, we turn to Matthew's account of the appearance of the risen Jesus in Galilee. Matthew echoes Mark's emphasis upon the central role of the women (27:55–56; 28:1–10) but the climax of his account focuses upon the encounter of the Eleven with Jesus. As so often in Matthew's Gospel, this key incident takes place upon a mountain, reinforcing the sacred and revelatory nature of what is taking place.

The theme of Jesus' kingship returns as he comes to them and declares, 'All authority in heaven and on earth has been given to me' (v. 18). Once again, his words unmistakably echo the vision of Daniel 7:13–14, where 'one like a son of man' was seen approaching 'the Ancient of Days' and was 'given dominion, glory and kingship'. Just a few days ago, we noted Jesus' use of this Danielic imagery when he stood before the Sanhedrin and claimed that *he* would be given this authority (Mark 14:62; Matthew 26:64). There he was claiming to be Israel's representative king, the one who would fulfil the nation's vocation to suffer and receive vindication, and here Jesus confirms his resulting authority over the whole created order. These words take us back to Matthew's account of the temptations, where the devil took Jesus up another high mountain and offered him 'all the kingdoms of the world and their splendour' in return for worshipping him (4:8–9). Jesus refused to accept this power because it meant sidestepping his vocation to fulfil Israel's charge to 'worship the Lord your God, and serve only him' (4:10). Now, through his ministry and death, Jesus has fulfilled this vocation and he may rightly accept the 'royal' authority that God has revealed and granted to him through the resurrection.

The command that the risen Jesus gives to his followers is to proclaim and assert this sovereign authority by inviting the peoples of every nation to become his followers. This entails baptizing them in the name of the Father, the Son and the Holy Spirit and teaching them to obey his commands (vv. 19–20). The resurrection of Jesus demonstrates that his kingly reign over this world has begun, since it shows the decisive conquest of evil and death by his love and life. Spreading the good news of Jesus is about showing this to be true and making it clear that coming under his protection and authority is open to everyone.

3 Sharing in the gift to the risen king

Acts 2:14–41

The explosive energy of the early Church requires an explanation. The crucial factor was their belief in Jesus' resurrection and their understanding of its significance for both Jesus and his followers. These early Christians found that the most natural way to express this significance was through the use of 'royal' terminology, as Jesus' resurrection became the lens through which all their experience was interpreted.

Peter's message to the crowds in Jerusalem on the Day of Pentecost is just one example of this. The Holy Spirit has suddenly come upon the believers (2:2–13) and Peter's explanation of this begins by quoting from the prophet Joel to show the eschatological nature of what has just occurred. In this prophecy, God had promised that 'in the last days… I will pour out my Spirit upon all flesh' (v. 17) and Joel spoke of this being confirmed by both charismatic experiences coming upon individuals (vv. 17b–18) and apocalyptic 'portents in the heaven above and signs on the earth below' (vv. 19–20). Peter then seeks to show that this experience has occurred only through the agency of Jesus and the power of his resurrection. God has initiated these 'last days' through 'the deeds of power, wonders, and signs' that he had done through Jesus of Nazareth, culminating in his resurrection when 'God raised him up, having freed him from death' (vv. 22–24).

The link between Jesus' resurrection and the pouring out of God's Spirit is then clarified by drawing upon the motif of kingship. Using Psalm 16, Peter shows how King David cannot have been referring to himself when he spoke of God's promise that the king would avoid 'corruption' and being 'abandoned to Hades' (vv. 25–32). Psalm 110 is used to make a similar point about the king's exaltation to God's right hand (vv. 34–35). Both must have been references to 'one of his descendants on the throne' (v. 30)—to Jesus of Nazareth, whom God had decisively shown to be the messianic king by raising him from the dead (v. 36). It is as this exalted king that Jesus has received the gift of the Holy Spirit, promised in Joel's prophecy, and poured it out on these people in Jerusalem (v. 33).

The value of this kingship motif is the way it expresses that what is given to Jesus the Messiah is passed on to his followers. A military victory in the ancient world was not just good news for the king but also for his army, which would share the spoils. Following 'the name' of someone who then became king was similarly advantageous. God's declaration through the resurrection that Jesus has been made 'Lord and Messiah' has a similar outcome because what he receives—in this case, the Spirit—is then poured out on everyone. This is why Peter stresses the importance of baptism so much in the early chapters of Acts. Baptism incorporates us into the benefits given to Jesus because it involves turning away from the rule of the world and coming under the rule of Jesus, God's appointed king.

4 The gospel of the risen king

Romans 1:1–7

The kingship of Jesus has rarely been seen as central to Paul's theology. This is partly because of a tendency to underestimate the thoroughly Jewish nature of the 'apostle of the Gentiles'. Another factor has been the willingness to believe that, within 20 years, 'Christ' had become a kind of surname for Jesus, completely detached from its original context.

This passage, at the start of Paul's most famous letter, suggests otherwise. Paul's gospel was completely grounded in Jewish thought, being promised by God 'beforehand through his prophets in the holy scriptures' (v. 2). Furthermore, it centred upon 'his Son, who was descended from David according to the flesh and was declared to be Son of God with power according to the spirit of holiness by resurrection from the dead, Jesus Christ our Lord' (vv. 3–4). This summary of the 'gospel' is therefore remarkably similar to that proclaimed at Pentecost by Peter. Jesus of Nazareth was of Davidic descent but the crucial factor in establishing his kingly credentials was his resurrection. This, according to Paul, was the decisive point at which God declared Jesus to be the holder of all the royal titles given to Israel's king—Son of God, Messiah/Christ and Lord.

Paul's background as a Pharisee is important here. Central to Pharisaic thought was the conviction that there would be a future resurrection, when God would raise and vindicate 'the righteous' in Israel. Paul's experience of the risen Jesus (Acts 9; 1 Corinthians 15:8) convinced him that this hope had been fulfilled in this one man. Jesus was therefore Israel's Messiah, who alone deserved the title 'Son of God'.

Verses 3–4 are therefore far from being Paul's polite acknowledgment of the Romans' beliefs before proceeding to his own rather different theology. They express convictions that were central to both Paul's theology and his personal vocation. Israel had completely failed to fulfil her calling to be the obedient 'son of God' whose faithfulness would witness to the Gentiles. The very opposite had occurred (Romans 2:17–24). This vocation had therefore been undertaken by Jesus, Israel's Messiah or anointed representative, who fulfilled it through his faithfulness (3:22) and who had been vindicated through his resurrection. Verses 5–7 anticipate the rest of the letter by showing that everyone who belongs to the Messiah receives both grace and peace from God. Like Paul, we also receive the commission to proclaim this kingship and 'bring about the obedience of faith among the Gentiles for the sake of his name' (v. 5). Followers of the risen king seek to bring others under his kingship.

5 Baptized into the risen king

Romans 6:1–14

This section of Romans shows the importance of Paul's 'royal theology' for Christian ethics. He is addressing why believers should lead moral lives when they have received 'the free gift of righteousness' through 'the one man, Jesus Christ' (5:17). If this grace comes exclusively through Jesus, then why shouldn't Christians 'continue in sin in order that grace may abound' (v. 1)?

Paul's response is completely grounded in the 'royal' significance of baptism. As we have seen, Jesus understood his suffering and death to be representative because he was fulfilling the vocation of Israel. Like Peter, Paul saw this royal claim as vindicated through the resurrection (1:4). This passage shows Paul's similar certainty that baptism incorporates the believer into every dimension of Jesus' death and resurrection. At Pentecost, Peter spoke of how baptism 'in the name of Jesus Christ' brought a sharing in the gift of the Holy Spirit given to the exalted king. Here, Paul concentrates upon the fact that 'the baptized' share in their king's death and resurrection and the moral consequences of this incorporation.

Paul immediately reminds the Romans that 'all of us who have been baptized into Christ Jesus were baptized into his death' (v. 3), and much of what follows expounds the meaning of this. At their baptism, believers were plunged below water, symbolizing their burial with Jesus (v. 4) and that their 'old self was crucified with him' (v. 6). We have seen how, through his death, Jesus endured the full consequences of Israel's sin, and Paul clearly understood this to have destroyed the power of sin over all those who had 'died' with him (vv. 6–7). This 'death' means that believers are also incorporated into Jesus' resurrection. Not only does this mean that those who are 'in Christ' can expect one day to live with him (v. 8) but it has important ethical implications. The resurrection was God's sign that death had lost its power over Jesus. His death to sin was therefore 'once and for all' since he now lives in God (vv. 9–10). Paul therefore insists that the lives of all those who belong to the king reflect this change of dominion. They must consider themselves 'dead to sin and alive to God in Christ Jesus' (v. 11).

Being 'in King Jesus' therefore means recognizing and seeking to live out what is proclaimed in our baptism. Freedom from sin is not just a legal acquittal requiring our gratitude. It is the transfer from one realm into another, a transfer from being under the rule of sin to being under the rule of God through his king. The imperative of Christian ethics therefore springs from the need to make our lives reflect this change of dominion. Soldiers in the ancient world presented their weapons to their king as a sign that they were loyal and would fight for him. In a similar manner, Paul calls all of us who are baptized 'to present your members to God as instruments of righteousness' (v. 13).

6 The triumphant reign of the risen king

1 Corinthians 15:20–28

This passage forms part of Paul's most sustained treatment of the resurrection. Other sections within this chapter deal with the scepticism that some of the Corinthian Christians had expressed about the possibility of such an event. Paul therefore shows how their faith and practice make sense only if their resurrection is guaranteed (15:12–19, 29–34) and he also includes details on the nature of their future transformed bodies (15:35–49). Within today's reading, however, his focus is on the resurrection of Jesus and its significance within the overall plan of God.

Once again, Paul's 'royal' understanding of Jesus as the Messiah forms the basis of his exposition. Jesus' role is that of an inclusive representative and, as in Romans 5, Paul explains this by drawing a parallel with Adam. Just as Adam's representative nature meant that death came through him to every human being, so the Messiah's role as a representative means that everyone who belongs to him will also be raised (vv. 20–22). This is why the Messiah has been raised first, because he is to lead the way as the 'first fruits of those who have died' (v. 20).

However, Paul's understanding of the significance of Jesus' resurrection goes deeper than this. It signals the beginning of Jesus' eschatological reign, with its purpose of defeating evil and reordering the world. In this connection, he quotes from Psalm 110, with its assertion that the king would be placed at God's right hand until all his enemies were placed under his feet (v. 27). During the Messiah's reign, every other ruler, authority and power will be gradually destroyed until the point of his royal arrival, his coming, when death will be the last enemy that is destroyed (v. 26). The climax of this whole process is the point where the Son will hand the kingdom over to God the Father

(v. 24). Once everything has been made subject through the Messiah, the Son himself will be made subject to the Father so that the whole process of cosmic reordering is complete, 'so that God may be all in all' (v. 28).

The resurrection of Jesus the Messiah has therefore set in motion the process by which the whole world will one day be put right. Every time that evil is vanquished should be seen as another victory of the risen king and his reign that will one day lead to the total destruction of all evil and death.

Guidelines

The uniqueness of Jesus rests upon the truth of his resurrection. Our identity and calling as his followers rest upon his kingship and the baptism that brought us under his rule. Use these words to ponder on the security and challenge that come from being baptized in the name of Jesus the king.

God raised King Jesus from the dead and sent the Holy Spirit to bring all the world to the kingdom of heaven. In baptism we die in sin and rise in newness of life in the king. Here we find rebirth in the Spirit, and set our minds on his heavenly gifts. As children of God, the king has given us a new dignity and he calls us live out this fullness of life.

FURTHER READING

M. Hooker, *The Message of Mark*, Epworth Press, 1983.

G. Kuhrt, *Believing in Baptism*, Mowbray, 1987.

T. Smail, *Once and For All*, Darton, Longman & Todd, 1998.

N.T. Wright, *The Resurrection of the Son of God*, SPCK, 2003.

N.T. Wright, *What St Paul Really Said*, Lion, 1997.

DANIEL

Daniel 1—6 consists of stories about Daniel and his three companions. The setting is Babylon, where these young men lived in exile after they had been taken there by King Nebuchadnezzar. Although some conservative scholars think that the stories relate historical events, there are strong reasons for holding that, just as Jesus taught by telling parables, so these stories were made up because this was a good way to teach. The stories contain a number of inaccuracies. For example, Belshazzar is said to have been a king and to have been on the throne when 'Darius the Mede' captured Babylon (5:1, 30–31), while Daniel 5:11, 18 and 22 state that Nebuchadnezzar was his father. But Belshazzar is never called 'king' in Babylonian records, and his father, who was Nabonidus and not Nebuchadnezzar, was king when Babylon was captured—not by Darius, but by Cyrus the Persian.

More important are incredible features of the stories. For example, a strict Jew such as Daniel could never have become one of the wise men of Babylon (2:13) and have been made 'chief prefect' over them (2:48), since the work done by such men was inextricably connected with Babylonian religion.

Daniel 7—12 (apart from the prayer in 9:3–19) relates visions that are written from the standpoint of a Daniel who lived in the sixth century BC. The prediction of the future in Daniel 11 is very detailed, and until 11:39 it is easy to tell what events are being described. Daniel 11:21–39 deals with the reign of Antiochus Epiphanes (175–164BC), down to 167BC, but 11:45 says that he will die in Palestine, though in fact he died in a campaign against the Parthians. Therefore, 11:45 must have been written before news of this reached Palestine, but after 167BC.

It is thought that the book of Daniel that appears in Protestant Bibles was completed between 167 and 164BC, though other Christian traditions recognize some later additions to Daniel (for example, Bel and the Dragon) as scripture. The beginning and end of Daniel are written in Hebrew, but the language changes to Aramaic (which was a *lingua franca* in the Middle East from around 700 to 200BC) in the middle of 2:4, and Aramaic continues to be used until 7:28. Thus, the changes in language do not correspond with the change from stories to visions, and these facts can probably best be accounted for if the whole of the book was not written at one time.

Daniel 1—6

1 In an alien land

Daniel 1:1–16

Though the date in 1:1 is unlikely to be correct, these tales are set in exile in Babylonia in challenging circumstances. 'The land of Shinar' (v. 2) is Babylonia, and this name is also used for Babylonia in the story of the tower of Babel (Genesis 11:2): it may have been chosen here to recall that story. Though Daniel and his companions make a success of life at the Babylonian court, there is a dark side to what is related. They have been uprooted from their own land, and have to do what their captors tell them. When they are taught 'the literature and language of the Chaldeans' (v. 4), they are being initiated into an alien culture. The word 'Chaldeans' can simply mean 'Babylonians', but it can also (as in Daniel 2:2) refer to a class of wise men, and it is widely supposed that this is the case here. The exiles did not only learn a new language, but had to become part of a strange new society. The giving of new names to Daniel and his companions (v. 7) is intended to help them assimilate, but is also a sign of their subordination. Daniel, however, rebels, and resolves 'that he would not defile himself with the royal rations of food and wine' (v. 8).

No completely satisfactory explanation of the reasons for this decision has been given. The food laws in the Old Testament would certainly not have been observed by those who worked in the palace kitchens but, though this could explain Daniel's refusal to eat the palace food, it leaves unexplained his refusal to drink the king's wine, since these laws say nothing about wine. More significant is Daniel's determination to make a stand on a matter that could be dangerous (v. 10) but seems to be related in some way to his religious beliefs, since the word 'defile' is used elsewhere in the Old Testament of ritual defilement.

We should pray that we become aware of and sensitive to the feelings and attitudes of those whose cultural background differs from ours.

2 The king's test

Daniel 2:1–12

A fondness for lists is a feature of the style of these stories, and the four names for interpreters of omens in verse 4 are included to make it clear that all the wise men of Babylon were summoned. The king's demand that they tell him what he has dreamt seems absurd, though Croesus, King of Lydia (c. 560–546BC), tested seven oracles by asking them to state what he was doing on the day his enquiry was made, and the oracle of Apollo at Delphi gave a correct answer (Herodotus, *Histories*, I. 46–48). Distrust of diviners lies behind both stories. This can be documented from Assyrian sources (that is, sources from Mesopotamia which are earlier than the reign of Nebuchadnezzar) and also from later Greek sources. There was ample room for dishonesty on the part of diviners, who might support one party at court against another, or even have an agenda of their own.

It would perhaps be wrong to assume that the stories of Daniel 1—6 were not intended to entertain: tales that grip the imagination can be a very effective way of teaching. In this passage, the theme of the distrust of diviners has been developed, with much exaggeration, to prepare for Daniel's success in relating and interpreting the dream, by emphasizing both that the other diviners cannot do as the king demands, even to save their lives, and that only the gods have such powers (v. 11). The diviners might have been expected to consult their gods, but they do not attempt this; the author would have been certain that the gods, like the diviners, would not have been able to pass the king's test.

We should pray that we as individuals, and organizations to which we belong, may be known for our integrity.

3 The true source of wisdom

Daniel 2:13–28a

We are told that 'in every matter of wisdom and understanding concerning which the king inquired of [Daniel and his companions], he found them ten times better than all the magicians and enchanters in his whole kingdom' (1:20). This theme of the superiority of Daniel's wisdom recurs in chapters 2, 4 and 5. Clearly, in real life it would have been absurd for the king to order the execution of 'all the wise men of Babylon' (2:12) before he had consulted the four men who might have been expected to have the best chance of passing his test, but in the story their absence when the others are consulted makes the contrast between their success and the other diviners' failure sharper. Similar literary devices are used in chapters 4 and 5 for the same reason.

In Mesopotamia, a diviner who needed to interpret a dream might ask a god to reveal the interpretation in another dream. Thus, Daniel is following a standard procedure, although, in accordance with the king's demand, he also requests information about the dream. It would have been perfectly reasonable had the wise men of Babylon told the king that they wanted to consult the gods, and, since Daniel was given time to pray to his God, they would presumably have been allowed to do this. Perhaps they panicked when faced with something that seemed to be impossible. In any case, their powerlessness is contrasted with the ability of Daniel's God to reveal to him what he needs to know.

When we run into difficulties, prayer should go hand in hand with taking appropriate advice and trying to think things through carefully. Laying things before God can help us to face an issue honestly (after all, we are never going to deceive God!) and can also, by bringing God into the situation, make it easier to handle. But we should not expect to receive an instant solution, as Daniel did.

4 Steadfast in adversity

Daniel 3:1–18

Daniel does not appear in this story. While it would be possible to think up some reason why the 'ruler over the whole province of Babylon' (2:48) should have been absent from an important occasion at which 'all the officials of the provinces' were present (3:2), it is frequently assumed that this story originally circulated independently of the stories about Daniel. Since four of the titles of officials in verse 2 are Persian words, but there are no Greek titles, the story was probably composed in the Persian period, between 539 and 331BC.

Shadrach, Meshach and Abednego take a stand that would have been unintelligible to most of Nebuchadnezzar's subjects, who believed in the existence of many gods and for whom a refusal to worship the god whose statue Nebuchadnezzar had erected would have seemed perverse obstinacy. 'Certain Chaldeans', who are presumably present because they are officials, denounce 'the Jews' (v. 8), saying to Nebuchadnezzar, 'There are certain Jews...' (v. 12). It has been suggested that this is a piece of early evidence for anti-Semitism. Shared religious worship was one of the things that bound a society together, so refusing to worship the image set up by Nebuchadnezzar was an extremely serious offence. The three men rudely address the king as 'Nebuchadnezzar' (v. 16), and not as 'King Nebuchadnezzar', so stressing the independent line they are taking. They question the king's belief that there is no god who can deliver them, though they admit that they may not be delivered (vv. 15, 17–18). It was no doubt well-known to the author that there were many occasions when God did not deliver those who were faithful to him. The three men take their stand on a matter of principle, and are willing to accept the consequences.

In 1998, ten statues of martyrs of the 20th century were placed over the west door of Westminster Abbey. Archbishop Luwum of Uganda, Martin Luther King and Dietrich Bonhoeffer are three of these martyrs. We should pray for Christians whose witness today puts them at serious risk.

5 Nebuchadnezzar's lesson

Daniel 3:19–30

A miracle would in any case have been needed to save the lives of the three men, but the author embellishes the story with details that heighten the sense of drama. The furnace is 'heated up seven times more than was customary' and its 'raging flames killed' the guards who threw the three men into it (vv. 19, 22). But the men, who had been bound before they were thrown into the furnace, are seen 'unbound, walking in the middle of the fire', and when they leave the furnace not only are they and their clothes unharmed but 'not even the smell of fire came from them' (vv. 21, 25, 27). A fourth man who 'has the appearance of a god' and who is later said to be an angel (vv. 25, 28) is with them in the furnace, but plays no other part in the story. A marginal note in the

NRSV says that the Aramaic phrase translated 'a god' is, translated literally, 'a son of the gods'. In both Aramaic and Hebrew, 'a son of such-and-such' can mean 'belonging to such-and-such a group', and 'a son of the gods' is a supernatural being of some kind. The polytheist Nebuchadnezzar at first calls him a god, but then, in conformity with the monotheistic standpoint of the author, says that he is an angel.

Nebuchadnezzar is understandably so impressed by what has happened that he issues a decree protecting the worship of 'the God of Shadrach, Meshach, and Abednego' (v. 29) but, though he says 'Blessed be' their God (v. 28), he does not say that he will worship him. The decree may be further evidence of anti-Jewish feeling. To their contemporaries it seemed not only extremely odd but also sacrilegious that Jews rejected the worship of all the gods except one, who was worshipped by no one else. Jews wanted respect for their distinctive religious position from their contemporaries, and Nebuchadnezzar gives them this.

How far do we respect the religious beliefs of those who disagree with us, and are there occasions when we should challenge any of these beliefs?

6 Hubris

Daniel 5:1–8, 17–31 (or 5:1–31)

When Nebuchadnezzar brought the sacred vessels to Babylon from the temple at Jerusalem, he treated them with respect (1:2). Belshazzar, by contrast, commits sacrilege by having them fetched so that he and his guests might drink from them while praising 'the gods of gold and silver, bronze, iron, wood, and stone' (vv. 2–4). The worshippers of these gods would have believed that the images represented their gods, but the Old Testament regularly claims that the images *are* the gods, so a contrast can be drawn between inanimate objects and the God who is active in creation and history (v. 23).

God responds at once to Belshazzar's impiety, but the wise men of Babylon cannot read or interpret what the mysterious hand writes. This may be because Aramaic, like Hebrew, was originally written without vowels. A cryptic message of only four words might well be un-intelligible unless its interpretation was known, since it might be possible to read it in several different ways. Daniel reads out the names of three weights: the mina, which weighed approximately 600 grammes; the shekel, which was one-fiftieth of a mina; and the parsin, which was either half a mina or half a shekel. These names are interpreted by means of a play on words that sound similar—for mina, the verb 'to number'; for shekel, the verb 'to weigh'; and for parsin, both the verb 'to break in two' and the name 'Persia'. This is a message of divine judgment, which is carried out 'that very night' (v. 30). Belshazzar has brought the judgment on himself, and Daniel makes it clear that he should have learnt from the way God disciplined his 'father' Nebuchadnezzar (vv. 18–22, compare ch. 4), instead of sinning more than his father did.

Perhaps the cultivation of a genuine concern for other people that always wishes their good is one way of guarding against hubris.

Guidelines

Some Jews genuinely think that in Britain the media are anti-Semitic but that they disguise this prejudice as support for the Palestinian cause. Some Muslims think that the Christian West is deliberately targeting Muslim countries. Events in the Middle East are seen in very different ways by different groups, and racial or religious prejudice is often thought to determine the way in which other groups see things. We all belong to some particular group, and this helps mould our attitudes. It is of the utmost importance that we should try to understand the point of view of other people, especially when we disagree strongly with them, and that we should do so as far as possible without making judgments in advance. We should endeavour above all to find out why others think as they do.

We should also beware of unthinkingly expressing derogatory attitudes by our actions. Institutional racism permeates the life of an institution without being noticed. Moreover, those who belong to a different race or religion often sense a snub where none is intended. In the end, it all boils down to having sympathy and respect for other people. This can be very rewarding, and can enrich our own lives, as well as contributing to the health of society.

Daniel 7—12

1 Kingdoms hostile to God

Daniel 7:1–8

The obvious question to ask is, what do these 'four great beasts' stand for? It is equally important, however, to consider what associations the imagery would have had when the chapter was written. The sea symbolizes the forces of chaos, and 'the four winds of heaven' (that is, winds from the four points of the compass) churn it up (v. 2) and so bring out more clearly its hostile character. The four beasts stand for four successive world empires and, although the first three beasts are distinguished sharply from the fourth beast, they all come up 'out of the sea' (v. 3). Thus, all four represent a flawed world order.

It is widely agreed that the beast 'like a lion' represents the Babylonian empire, the beast 'that looked like a bear' the Median empire, the beast 'like a leopard' the Persian empire, and the 'fourth beast' the Greek empires of Alexander the Great and his successors. The inclusion of the Median empire is probably due to knowledge of the predictions in Isaiah 13:17–22 and Jeremiah 51:11–14 that the Medes would destroy Babylon. This did not happen, and there was no Median empire that supplanted the Babylonian empire. It has been suggested that the fourth beast is an elephant, but no specific animal need be in mind. Its precise appearance may have been left to the imagination.

We tend to think of the Greeks as the bringers of culture; here they are portrayed as significantly more brutal than their predecessors. Horns symbolized strength (compare 1 Kings 22:11), and stand here for kings who ruled the Jews. Ten may well be a round number, so these kings cannot be identified, but the 'little' horn (v. 8), so called to disparage him, is Antiochus Epiphanes (175–164BC). His policies were perceived by the Jews as an attack on their religion and culture, though they lived on the southern boundary of his empire and his main concern may have been to strengthen his hold over a people whose loyalty might be uncertain.

In different ways, all four empires are found wanting. Should such a negative estimate of earthly power contribute to our thinking today? If so, does it tell the whole story?

2 God intervenes

God, represented as a white-haired old man, sits on his throne to judge the four beasts, and innumerable angels are in attendance (vv. 9–10). The arrogance of the little horn is such that the fourth beast is put to death.

Chapter 7 was presumably composed between 167 and 164BC in response to Antiochus Epiphanes' attack on the Jewish religion. It is often said that the author believed that God had to act in the face of such wickedness. Verse 12 is puzzling, since the four kingdoms rule one after another, and the first three have disappeared when the fourth is established. The first three empires do not, however, deserve as severe a punishment as the fourth, and they would be included among those who serve the 'one like a human being' (v. 13). The NRSV margin notes that this is what is meant by the Aramaic 'one like a son of man'. It has often been held that he is the Messiah, but the author(s) of Daniel do not seem to be expecting a messianic king. The book says a great deal about the establishing of a new world order which will be everlasting, but the verb 'to anoint' and the noun 'anointed one' are found only three times in Daniel, in 9:24–26. The NIV finds a reference to the Messiah in 9:25–26, but notes the non-messianic interpretation of these verses in the margin. It is certain that the 'one like a son of man' of 7:13 was thought to be the Messiah some 150 years after this chapter was written, but if the author(s) of Daniel had expected a Messiah, they would surely have given him a major place in chapters 7—12. The message of the vision is that a heavenly judgment will deliver those Jews who had been faithful to God from their enemies, and that a new world order, which will ensure their security for ever, will be established.

By now many Christians no longer expect the imminent return of Christ, which is the equivalent for us of the establishment of a new world order. It is assumed that we will make the planet uninhabitable in the relatively near future, or that life will be wiped out as the result of a collision with an object from outer space, or that life will go on indefinitely. We are challenged to find a place in our thinking for the belief that everything is in the hand of God and that ultimately he will sort out the mess we make of his world.

3 Interpreting the vision

Daniel 7:15–28

The last book in the New Testament, which contains material similar to the visions in Daniel, is sometimes called 'The Apocalypse'. The word 'apocalypse' means 'revelation' or 'disclosure', and Daniel 7 and writings like it are known as apocalyptic. In some ways, apocalyptic continues the work done earlier by the prophets, but there are also significant differences between the prophetic books and Daniel. For example, the prophets' message includes a call to repentance and the promise that, if the people repent, the disaster threatened as a punishment will be averted. By contrast, Daniel provides information about what has been decided about the future, and those who read or hear it must adapt to it.

Another characteristic of apocalyptic is that a revelation is given to someone by an angel. In the interpretation of Daniel's vision, hardly anything is said about the first three beasts. It is clear that the writer is primarily interested in the fourth beast and what will happen after it has been judged, when 'the holy ones of the Most High' will receive a kingdom that will last for ever (vv. 18, 22). In the vision, the 'one like a human being' stands for these holy ones, who are frequently thought to be the faithful Jews who had resisted Antiochus Epiphanes. The main purpose of the vision is to assure them that the tribulations they were suffering would soon come to an end, and that God would then establish a kingdom unlike any previous kingdom, in which they would rule over all the earth (v. 27). There is very little detailed description of what this kingdom will be like. Nothing is said about the end of the world, and world history is important only as it affects the Jews. The kingdom is to be set up on earth (v. 27), but it is not just a continuation of what has happened previously. An entirely new order of things will replace the present world order.

Christians have taken seriously the petitions 'thy kingdom come, thy will be done on earth as it is in heaven', and have tried to advance the setting up of God's kingdom on earth, but little progress has been made. Will the establishment of such a kingdom ever be possible?

4 Angels

Daniel 10:4–9, 15—11:1 (or 10:4—11:1)

The description of an angel in verses 5–6 draws heavily on imagery found in the book of Ezekiel. The angel is generally assumed to be Gabriel (compare 8:16; 9:21). It is hardly surprising that Daniel is terrified when he sees the angel and has to be reassured. The angel has come to tell Daniel 'what is inscribed in the book of truth' (v. 21), and this is disclosed in 11:2—12:3.

Chapter 10 mentions another function that some angels have. We are familiar with the expression 'a guardian angel', though nowadays most people do not believe that such angels really exist. Jesus was speaking about guardian angels when he said that the angels of children 'continually see the face of my Father in heaven' (Matthew 18:10). This implies a close link between the earthly and the heavenly, and, for the author(s) of Daniel, what happened in the heavenly realm was of crucial importance because it mirrored what happened on earth. 'The prince of Persia', 'the prince of Greece' and 'Michael, your prince' (vv. 20–21) are the patron angels of the various countries. This vision was ostensibly seen during the reign of 'King Cyrus of Persia' (10:1), and Gabriel will soon have to return to fight with Michael against the patron angel of Persia. It is interesting to find this active hostility against the Persians on the part of the Jews, though this need not mean actual fighting on earth. It would have been thought that the end of the Persian empire must be accompanied by activity in heaven. It will be replaced by the Greek empire, with whose patron angel Gabriel and Michael will then fight (vv. 20–21).

Such heavenly activity is foreign to our way of thinking, and many Christians are unsure whether angels exist, but the question about how the heavenly interacts with the earthly is raised for anyone who believes in God. Christianity claims not only that God created the world but that he also maintains it in being. We can see in this a co-operation between God and the world that enables him to participate in events on earth.

5 History under God's control

Daniel 11:2–39 outlines the history of the Near East as it affected the Jews from the time of the Persian kings until 167BC. None of the rulers is named, and it is uncertain which four Persian kings are meant (v. 2). The 'warrior king' (v. 3) is Alexander the Great, who overran Persia in 330BC, but who died in 323BC. After his death, his empire was eventually divided into four kingdoms (v. 4). 'The king of the south' is Ptolemy I of Egypt, and the officer (v. 5) is Seleucus I, who was driven out of Babylonia and became one of Ptolemy's generals, but who recaptured Babylon and created the largest of the four kingdoms that succeeded Alexander's.

In due course, the accession of Antiochus Epiphanes is reached (v. 21). He was not the rightful heir, and 'the prince of the covenant' who is killed (v. 22) is the high priest Onias III, who was murdered around 171BC. The account of Epiphanes' reign up to 167BC (vv. 21–39) and predictions about how his reign would end (11:40—12:1) are the point to which this recital of history leads.

Past history is probably related at such length to indicate that everything happened in accordance with a divine plan. Whatever might seem to be the case, God was in charge, and the climax of history had been reached. God would intervene and act decisively against the king who will 'consider himself greater than any god', but who will prosper only 'until the period of wrath is completed' (v. 36). This is the period during which the Jews would be at the mercy of Epiphanes, but it is made clear that a fixed term is set for this. Compare 7:25, where the holy ones 'shall be given' (note the passive) into his power for three and a half years. Thus, it is claimed that the course of history is predetermined.

Some Christians believe in predestination and others do not, but, even if the events of history have not been predetermined, it can still be maintained that God is in charge. There are also ways in which we are all subtly influenced by circumstances outside our control—for example, by the attitudes of our family and friends. There is some truth in predestination, even if we reject the doctrine in its fullest form.

6 Resurrection

It is safe to assume that 'the wise among the people' (11:33) include the author(s) of the visions in chapters 7—12. They have suffered at the hands of Antiochus Epiphanes, and some of them have been killed. It is often said that the 'little help' that they receive (11:34) is a disparaging reference to the rebellion against Epiphanes, which was led by the Maccabees and is described in 1 Maccabees. There is a 'time appointed' for the end of the tribulations suffered by the wise (11:35), and they must wait patiently for this. There will be 'a time of anguish' un-paralleled in human history, and then Michael, the patron angel of the Jews, will be the one who delivers them. But he delivers only those 'found written in the book' (12:1). It is normally supposed that this is the book of life (compare Malachi 3:16–18). During most of the Old Testament period there was no developed belief in life after death, and it was believed that everyone who died would enter upon an insubstantial, shadowy existence in the underworld, which was called Sheol (compare Isaiah 14:9–11). Daniel 12:2–3 is the only passage in the Old Testament that teaches a doctrine of resurrection and judgment.

Not everyone who has died will be raised, however. The author(s) are primarily concerned with 'those who are wise' (12:3), the group to which they belong. In Daniel 8:10 the stars stand for angels, and 12:3 may be saying that the righteous who are raised will be associated with the angels and share the life of heaven. In any case, they, like Daniel (12:13), will be raised to be rewarded. Those who 'awake… to shame and everlasting contempt' (12:2) are presumably conspicuous sinners who had not been punished adequately before they died. No information is given about the fate of ordinary Jews. Daniel 12 is moving away from the teaching of the rest of the Old Testament about the afterlife, in the direction of later Christian teaching, but this has not yet been reached.

We should pray that we may live as people who know that life on earth is not an end in itself.

Guidelines

These notes have been written from the standpoint of mainstream biblical study. Obviously, there is room for difference of opinion on points of detail, but there is widespread agreement that the book of Daniel does not contain prophecies that have still to be fulfilled. The author(s) who have given us this book as it appears in Protestant Bibles finished their work between 167 and 164BC (see the introduction above), and they included nothing that they thought would happen more than a few years ahead. Thus, speculations about the second coming and the end of the world based on Daniel are a misuse of scripture.

The thought-world of apocalyptic is alien territory. Since it has contributed to the New Testament, Christians today cannot ignore apocalyptic completely. The belief expressed in Daniel that God's kingdom would be established soon may be compared with the belief current in the early Church that the second coming was imminent. Neither expectation was correct, but both contain important insights. Daniel stresses that the powers of evil that appear to dominate the world are under judgment. The New Testament reminds us that the God who created the world has not abandoned it but will, in his own good time, bring to completion the work that he began at the creation. This approach to scripture uses it selectively, but that is what anyone who does not think that the Bible is infallible must do.

We should recognize that scripture does not always speak with the same voice, but even so it is not difficult to tell what the central truths of our faith are. The question then becomes, what else is there in scripture that is consistent with these tenets and that can be defended in the 21st century? Apocalyptic still has a contribution to make.

FURTHER READING

John J. Collins, *Daniel*, Hermeneia, Fortress Press, 1993. The best commentary on Daniel.

John E. Goldingay, *Daniel*, Word Biblical Commentary, Word Books, 1989. Good on the teaching of Daniel.

Ernest Lucas, *Daniel*, Apollos Old Testament Commentary, Apollos and InterVarsity Press, 2002. The best commentary from a conservative viewpoint.

Daniel L. Smith-Christopher, 'The Book of Daniel', in *The New Interpreter's Bible*, edited by Leander E. Keck and others, Volume VII, Abingdon Press, 1996, pp. 17–152. An interesting treatment by a Quaker.

PIONEERS OF AGE

'The situation is that my generation is a pioneering generation. My mother and father didn't live as long as I will, and I've no one to show me how to grow old—we are breaking new ground as older people. Who will show us the way?' This comment from an older woman several years ago challenged me to think more seriously about these issues, and eventually to write *Pioneering the Third Age*.

We are living through a unique event in history: never before have so many lived for so long. With increased longevity, to age 'successfully' for many is to age healthily and maintain activity for as long as possible. But in the quest for a youthful old age there is a cost as our present culture concentrates on the here and now—on activity, on achievement—and, through a creeping ageism where even older people deny the value of age, the value of the older person in society is lost.

Christians are not immune to these effects. We are right to reach out to younger generations with the good news of Christ Jesus, but we fail when we miss the huge mission field of older people with finite time remaining to hear the gospel. The next 14 days are aimed at beginning to recover the value and the voice of the older person in scripture, and to see the plans and purposes God holds for us in older age. To this end, I'm most grateful to the contributors of the two 'Guidelines' sections, who have themselves reflected on what it means to be an older person in light of a life journeying heavenwards, and have allowed me to share their thoughts with you.

Quotations are taken from the New International Version of the Bible.

18–24 APRIL

Old Testament

1 Abraham and Sarah: the God of all age

Genesis 17:1–22

A key moment in history: God reveals himself to Abram and initiates an amazing covenant relationship expressed in the sign of circumcision, seen in the change of a name, confirmed with the birth of a son and guaranteed to future generations. Talk about a whirlwind of change! And all this happens to a man aged 99 and his wife aged 90. No wonder it all seemed a bit incomprehensible, especially the bit about having a child at their stage of life! What limitations had age brought to Abraham and Sarah? One we know for certain was that they were past the age of child-bearing, and they were probably both experiencing increasing frailty in their old age. The theologian Walter Brueggemann observes that 'Abraham and especially Sarah are not offered here as models of faith but as models of disbelief. For them, the powerful promise of God outdistances their ability to receive it'. God reveals to this older couple in their disbelief that our potential does not diminish with our age in God's sight, for he is God of all age and ages.

In contemporary society, older age can be thought of as two experiences—the third and fourth ages. The simplest description of these is that those in their third age experience some form of retirement, have a good level of mobility and manage their lives without outside assistance. People in their fourth age would be those who require physical assistance or care due to age-related disability, illness or frailty caused by the process of ageing. This is not to suggest that those experiencing their fourth age are in some way less than those in their third age. The third and fourth ages both contain the potential for the person to develop, to have expression and to receive respect.

Throughout Abraham's and Sarah's journey we read of a couple in whom respect of older age is not only given by God but is rediscovered by this older couple, who thought they were beyond usefulness in God's plans.

2 Naomi: inspiring others

Ruth 1:1–22

Far too often I have a read the story of Ruth and missed the story of Naomi. I have seen Ruth as an inspirational character who embraces the faith-identity of her mother-in-law, endures hardship and places her trust in the faithfulness of God. All this is true, but the vital question as Ruth inspires us is: who inspired Ruth?

Widowhood in antiquity often meant that, with the death of a husband, an older woman became even more vulnerable to old age, and Naomi's vulnerability is all too apparent with no husband and no sons to care for her. The risks she faced as an older woman were too great for her to involve her daughters-in-law. However, to view Naomi as merely the victim of the piece would be a mistake, for the book of Ruth reveals a great depth to the spirituality of the older person despite the afflictions that life may bring. Naomi's prayer (vv. 8–9) demonstrates her own commitment to care for the two young women, Orpah and Ruth, and while Naomi acknowledges her suffering, she still refers to God in personal terms as 'the Lord' (Yahweh) and 'the Almighty' (vv. 20–21).

The theme of Naomi's care-giving runs throughout Ruth's story, but it is at the very end of this short book that we read the outworking of inspired care continued by Naomi for the next generation: 'Then Naomi took the child, laid him in her lap and cared for him' (4:16). The interaction between Naomi and Ruth provides us with a powerful model of how an older woman not only inspired but, in many ways, mentored a younger woman. Naomi's desire to trust God despite her situation was combined with her concern for Ruth, and so we see Ruth's willingness to be inspired by this older woman. It is a story containing a vital challenge for us today—not to dismiss the older person as someone who is no longer relevant, but instead to honour him or her as a person who has lived life with and through God and who can inspire the younger person to do the same.

3 The wisdom of years

Psalm 71

The theologian Derek Kidner has described Psalm 71 as a psalm for old age. Its writer is facing the distress of oppression by enemies, but in old age suffering has befallen him. To those of his own time he has become a sign of the vicissitudes of ageing. We know that this is written by an older man because he tells us so in this psalm, which reflects not only the uncertainty of frailty but also the hope that only the wisdom of years can bring: 'For you have been my hope, O Sovereign Lord, my confidence since my youth' (v. 5).

Hindsight is a blessing. We are able to look back over past events and take time to learn from them, and this is wisdom in the making—learning from our own mistakes. The older one is, the greater the potential to consider the length of years lived. But for many people, that process of looking back can be combined with fears about vulnerability of age in the present, so clouding judgment. Then wisdom is lost as the past is mourned and the present resented. The situation of the psalmist is similar in nature to that of Naomi in the story of Ruth, age bringing with it vulnerability. But the psalmist, like Naomi, also holds a tremendous challenge for older people considering the whole of life and their present situation. The writer of this psalm does not blame God, reject God or deny God. Instead, in embracing his present situation he embraces God. Looking back over his life, he sees the way in which God has sustained and taught him since his youth. To the very day of writing, he can still declare God's marvellous deeds, and in doing so he embraces the future hope he has as he seeks the refuge of God.

This isn't an older man withdrawing into himself, however, counting down his remaining days. Through his gaze back over the horizon of the journey already travelled, he can see that a purpose still remains for him. He has a story of a journey filled with tales of God's goodness and faithfulness, and this is a story to be shared with the next generation. Recovering the voice of the wisdom of age and enabling it to be shared among us is vital if we are to learn lessons from the past and so avoid the repetition of mistakes.

4 'A prayer of Moses the man of God'

Psalm 90

This psalm has been described as one of the most magisterial of the psalms, spoken by a man of extraordinary nature and stature in Old Testament scripture. Imagine Moses standing at Pisgah, facing the promised land towards which he has been headed all his life. Yet he knows, standing on that mountain, that he will go no further; he will not enter that land, and his life will now end. In an amazing example of submission to the reality of God, he hands his hopes and dreams on to future generations.

Walter Brueggemann considers verse 12 to be the pivotal point of the psalm, as the psalm affirms that the goal of prayer, piety and spirituality is finally to have a wise heart. 'To number our days aright' and thus to 'gain a heart of wisdom' is something that can be discovered only with a life of 70 or 80 years (see v. 10). It is this wisdom of heart that enables us to hold the question 'Why?' in our hearts when we face difficult life situations. As we read in Psalm 71, such wisdom of years is a precious resource among us, for it enables us to hold the sorrows and trouble in context: they pass away and affect us but for a while.

But is growth in piety, prayer and spirituality something that is encouraged among older members of our churches? Are they qualities that we are all encouraged to explore at any stage in our process of ageing? If we can unlock these disciplines within our lives, we might reveal something of the treasure that is the heart of wisdom, as Moses discovered. His journey of life with the everlasting God and the continual development of that relationship, despite its ups and downs, meant that the older Moses knew that death could not rob him of what he had yet to see accomplished in his own lifetime. He would not complete his purposes; he wouldn't receive the accolade of leading the people into the promised land. Nevertheless, the experience of his journey of life with the everlasting God meant that Moses knew he could trust God's promises and leave in death that which was unfinished in his own temporal lifetime.

5 A reality check

Ecclesiastes 4:13; 12:1–7

It is easy to fall into the trap of believing the myth that as someone grows older they automatically grow wiser and increasingly holy, but Ecclesiastes 4:13 explodes that myth! Old age and wisdom do not necessarily develop together. For the writer of Ecclesiastes, it is obvious: it is precisely the mark of a wise man to take counsel, while the foolish believe there is nothing new they could be taught. As one gerontologist recently explained to me, ageism has a dreadful impact upon older people but one of the most ageist groups of people can be older people themselves.

There was a young trainee minister who took up a new post in a church. At a meeting of the church congregation, where people were being introduced, this young minister explained to all those present that during his training he had found that participants on his course older than himself had not taken him seriously because of his age. When he was offered the post of trainee minister at this large church, some of his older fellow trainees suggested that someone so 'young' should not take such a post. The purpose in sharing this experience had been to explain both where this trainee minister had come from and his hopes for his new role in the church where he now worked. Unfortunately, the trainee minister was followed by an older member of the church who declared that while what the trainee had said was of interest, the validity of his experience was to be doubted, because he was too young to understand such matters… Truly it is better to be a poor youth than an old and foolish king!

Ecclesiastes 12:1–7 brings us to the realities of older age, with its potential fears and frailty, as the writer sets out clearly the way in which old age leads to death. There is a clear realism to these verses, setting out the reality of the end of life. Death is truly the one thing of which we can be certain in this life, but how are we prepared for death? Perhaps part of the fear of older age is the individual's increasing realization of the finite nature of his or her life, and many who do not know the salvation of Jesus Christ face that realization depending on 'internal' rather than 'eternal' resources to enable them to approach the end of their journey in this life.

6 Dreaming dreams

Joel 2:28–32

Joel's prophecy, echoed by Peter in Acts 2, provides us with a helpful link as we complete this first week of looking at ageing in the Old Testament, and points us towards the New Testament. In these verses, Joel speaks of roles for both young and old in the day of the Lord: old men will dream dreams and young men will see visions. It is a wonderful picture of how distinctions of age, sex and social class were to be abolished through a common spiritual endowment witnessed at the foundation of the Church. In the Old Testament, the majority of references to the Spirit of God are in relation to his empowering of certain individuals for particular tasks. In this prophecy, however, God is speaking of empowering not a particular person or group of people, but all people, and there will be no discrimination as far as the activity of the Spirit is concerned in terms of age, sex or status.

When reflecting upon verse 28, I have always been struck by the difference in experience for young and old. The use of language here recognizes the experience that age brings with it. The young, through their lack of life experience, are dependent upon the provision of vision for what will be. The old, with lives full of experience, both positive and negative, have a wealth from which to draw in their dreams. It is a subtle distinction but vital if we are to see the value of all ages within the church being able to contribute to its life as a whole, while at the same time retaining generational distinctiveness of experience. This distinctiveness is a great blessing for us, but to recognize it we must work to encourage younger people in their desiring the use of spiritual gifts in their lives, while at the same time enabling the same for older people—giving value to their dreams of what could be with lives lived in Christ Jesus.

Guidelines

Today, Lord God, as I look back over my life's journey
my heart is full of thanksgiving and praise.
I know your protecting hand was upon me
from the moment of my birth.
When I was young and immature
you showed me the path that I should take.
As the storm clouds gathered and my world started to fall apart
you were a rock and a refuge to me;
a rock where my feet could find a firm foothold
when everything else was shifting,
a refuge where I could run for cover
when I was battered by pain, resentment and fear.

Lord God you have been a loving and faithful father to me,
but once again I stand in need of your reassurance.
I need to know that you will listen and that you will understand.
Don't put me on one side now that I am getting old;
my physical powers are beginning to fail;
sometimes my confidence disappears like a puff of smoke;
younger people see me as finished, of little value.
Lord God, be my refuge—my trust is in you.

I will always have hope because of who you are.
I will declare your love and faithfulness
to those who are just starting out on their journey.
I will tell them that you are a God who saves and rescues,
that you are a God of integrity whose favour lasts for a lifetime;
you are a rock for their feet and a secure foundation for their lives.
I will tell them that you are my God
and I will praise you to the end of my days.

A PSALM FOR THE THIRD AGE, BY MARGARET HOPKINSON (BASED ON PSALM 71)

New Testament

1 Elizabeth and Zechariah: when God surprises!

Luke 1:5–25, 39–45

Luke opens his Gospel with an older couple who have no children, and an amazing series of events. Zechariah, a Levite on priestly duty in the temple, has an encounter with an angel of the Lord, who tells him he is to become a father. Zechariah's response to this unexpected news is disbelief and so his mouth is sealed, preventing him from telling anyone of what had happened. Elizabeth, although advanced in years, becomes pregnant, and recognizes how God has removed from her the social disgrace of childlessness and, in doing so, has shown her his favour.

Who could ever have expected this series of events? Zechariah and Elizabeth certainly didn't.

What is the outcome of all this for our older couple? Well, for Zechariah it is the revelation that God still has clear purposes for him and his wife: filled with the Holy Spirit, his mouth is opened and he prophesies about the unborn child Jesus. For Elizabeth, there is an amazing role as an older woman: she is the first person in Luke's Gospel to recognize and declare the unborn Jesus as Messiah (v. 43). From the outset, Luke is in no doubt that older people have a vital role of witness and declaration in the kingdom of God. Too often, however, their voice is lost to us today as ageism creeps into our relationships and attitudes toward older people.

Ageism denies the contribution and value of older people within our society. It is a phenomenon that has many roots, including retirement. Retirement is a modern post-war construct that strips older men and women of value. For some people, retirement can be a time of opportunity, but for many it is a time of uncertainty and struggle to find purpose. It is in this struggle that Luke presents Zechariah. He had accepted that his time was over—there was nothing more for him to contribute except for his duties as priest, and even those would be limited as he aged. But, as Abraham and Sarah discovered in Genesis, God is the God of all time and ages.

If Zechariah teaches us never to underestimate what God can accomplish through the older person, through Elizabeth we should receive a healthy rebuke for any time when older women have been denied a place within the church. Here we read of the original first-century evangelist in full flow, declaring the Lordship of Jesus Christ— an evangelist who has spoken through 2000 years of history that flowed from this point.

2 Simeon and Anna: waiting patiently for God's time

Luke 2:22–38

Luke is keen to present credible witnesses to the Messiah, and following on from Zechariah and Elizabeth are Simeon and Anna in the temple in Jerusalem. Simeon was known as being righteous and devout, having been patiently waiting for the 'consolation of Israel', and Anna, widowed at an early age, had committed her life to God as a prophetess. What changes they must have seen and experienced in their lives—the occupation of their country by an oppressive force, the imposition of the rule of a puppet king—yet, in the midst of turbulence, their patient wait brings an oasis of calm in which they each behold a child. The promise of the Messiah had kept the hope of the nation alive, but how could Simeon and Anna so clearly recognize him when so many could not?

The process of ageing reveals the infinite nature of knowledge. As we grow older, the amount we know appears to be insignificant compared to the amount it is possible to know, so we must be prepared to embrace the uncertain vastness. Yet knowing Christ, recognizing his very presence, can provide an oasis of certainty. For Simeon and Anna, this was not a finished product, providing all the answers to life and the universe. It was simply this assurance: God keeps his promises. And for Simeon, it meant he could die knowing the simple truth revealed in the person of a child presented on a single day in his lifetime in the temple—that the light had come into the world and God's salvation was revealed.

I wonder if Simeon's and Anna's voices would be heard today. The voices of older people are so often lost in the cacophony of activity that can fill a church. With the rush of activity, we miss the oasis of calm, and that patient wait upon God becomes devalued as it is considered not to be accomplishing anything. May God forgive us for the times we have silenced these voices of older people, experienced in the ways of God and able to recognize his revelation to us today. Simeon's and Anna's voices echo down the centuries to us today; can we recognize not only what they say to us but their voice as older people?

3 The widow's example: living a joint account
Luke 20:45—21:4

As an older woman in the first century, you had little respect and few opportunities, and to be a widow meant adding vulnerability and the spectre of poverty to these difficulties. The writer Michael Apichella has recognized this older woman in Luke's Gospel as a hidden asset:

Where does one find the faith to act in this way? I believe that her faith grew over many years of trusting God to meet her needs—physical, mental and emotional. What's more, I believe that her faith was the result of a deep conviction that the Lord would not allow her charity to cause her to starve. To give away all that one has for God's sake is the act of a person who has had a long and nourishing relationship with God, a relationship that had been growing over many years.

I recently heard someone describe this older woman as being someone who lived a 'joint account' with God, that all she had was God's and vice versa—faith in action!

The story of this older woman is no parable, however: she is a living example in history. As Jesus was speaking to his disciples, he looked up and saw this woman going about something that she had most likely done many times before. It was no one-off event but part of her lifestyle.

The warning Jesus gives to his disciples about the teachers of the law devouring widows' houses (20:47) reveals both the difference in attitude of this older woman in comparison to teachers of the law, and the extent of the woman's potential vulnerability. Such teachers of the law were unable to charge for their teaching but, because of their supposed piety, would often be executors of estates left by husbands to provide for their wife. This role of executor provided an opportunity to increase the teacher's income through charging exorbitant fees for looking after the widows' estates.

It is dreadful to think that such a wonderful asset of God's kingdom could be abused in such a way. In our contemporary society, the issue of 'elder abuse' has only recently been recognized. It can take the form of physical, emotional, sexual, neglectful and financial abuses against the older person, who is often unable to take action as their vulnerability leaves them open to exploitation. Older people are an asset to a church, an asset that needs to be defended at times against the cruelties of others.

4 Jesus' example: care in crisis

John 19:25–27

There is no clear theme of teaching regarding older people in scripture. While Jesus points to older people as signs of the kingdom of God and Gospel writers hold them up as examples, there isn't a clear section in which Jesus deals with the issue of what it means to be concerned about the older person. Or is there? At the very heart of the events surrounding the life of Jesus is his crucifixion—it is the point from which redemption history flows—and here, at this crucial turning-point in the history of creation, comes an incredible compassion for a widowed older woman, Mary.

We have already seen the way in which older women, especially those who were widows, faced increased vulnerability in old age, but in the midst of the pain of crucifixion, both temporal and eternal, Jesus speaks words of concern for his mother. It is an incredible statement of care at a moment of crisis. It appears that Jesus' brothers and sisters were absent from the crucifixion scene, so as the firstborn son it was Jesus' prerogative to hand the care of his mother to the disciple John.

Throughout Jesus' teaching there runs a thread of inspired care and compassion in concern for the older person. It is a compassion he expressed in his death, and a compassion that was to be continued in the teachings of the early Church by his brother James. The issue of caring for vulnerable older people is a difficult subject in our fragmented society. Few extended families remain, and most people accept the need for mobility if they wish to have employment. The one extended family that does remain, however, is that of the church. It is a tremendous challenge, but how can we ensure that older people are not left in vulnerability? I do not know the final answer to such a question, but I know that the answer begins with my attitude towards the older person and my willingness to be Christ-like to people facing vulnerability.

5 Paul's view: relationships between the ages

1 Timothy 5:1–10

Little mention is made of old age in Paul's letters. There is speculation as to why this might have been the case. One suggestion has been that,

in its early missionary expansion, the energy of church leaders went primarily into evangelism and not discipleship. With the steady growth of the church and the passing of time, however, people and congregations aged and it was an issue that could no longer be avoided, especially as younger leaders like Timothy were appointed and led churches containing older people.

In his first letter to Timothy, Paul deals rapidly with a series of issues about older members of the church, but underlining all of this is the attitude with which Timothy was to carry out his duties. He was not to rebuke older members of the church by browbeating them into submission with the power and force of his argument. Rather, Paul instructs Timothy to encourage them, to use gentle persuasion, and in doing so treat older members with respect, dignity and honour. This did not mean that Timothy as a younger leader was to become a doormat, only ever displaying a 'welcome' sign to whatever an older person wanted to do in the church. But Paul's concern was for the way in which Timothy was to lead.

Paul was sharing with Timothy the benefit of his own experience as an older man. When we consider Paul's instructions to Timothy, we must hold in mind Paul's own concerns about leadership. Paul was the man who learnt that Christ's grace was sufficient for him and, in doing so, discovered power in weakness—an attitude that marks his letters with his compassion for people and passion for Jesus. But Paul did not keep these lessons to himself. Paul and Timothy were in relationship, the older man, Paul, encouraging and mentoring the younger man, Timothy.

Passing on the treasure of wisdom, knowledge and experience in leadership and life is a vital resource that the older person can offer to younger people. These relationships between older and younger can bring much fruit, but they require nurturing and encouragement if they are to happen. Such a practical outworking of relationships between older and younger people in the church is something that we don't celebrate very well, and it can pass us by without anyone noticing. How wonderful it would be to hear more older and younger people speaking about what a relationship/friendship in Christ had brought into their lives.

6 James' concern: Christ-inspired compassion

With this single verse we end our journey considering different portions of scripture, what they present to us about the process of ageing and the value of older people. Christ-inspired compassion finds expression in this pointed saying of James. It is a tough sentence to hear, containing great challenge in a few words. But James is using the word 'religion' positively, giving it both content and a practical outworking. He is not presenting a comprehensive definition of Christianity, but rather points us in the way that lives should be lived, which includes care for the vulnerable aged. William Booth, founder of the Salvation Army, ensuring both a practical content and outworking, said, 'We will wash [our money] in the tears of widows and orphans and lay it on the altar of humanity.'

Christ-like compassion is not to be reserved purely for the moment of crisis, when no one else can intervene, but is to run throughout the life of the person who calls himself or herself a 'Christian'. As we have seen over these last two weeks, from the inspired care of Ruth to the instruction of Jesus on the cross to his disciple, it is both a divine instruction to the individual to care for the older person and also a challenge to the older person to be an inspirer of care.

We cannot decline our responsibility or relationship to one another in Christ. Old or young, we are related to one another, and there is a need to care for each other, to recognize one another in the context of the body of Christ and to rejoice that in Christ we are united in the glorious promise of eternal life with him. An example that inspired me was an evening service where the service leader encouraged the younger people in the service to go and say 'thank you' to and pray with an older member of the church. It was inspirational because I looked around and saw people united in Christ, related to one another, looking beyond the outward appearances of age and rejoicing in God with one another.

Guidelines

We tend to judge people by their activity—in how much their business makes, how great their output is in writing or painting, how many goals they score, or what records they break. Hence, it may be no wonder if

135

old people feel a bit left out, even a failure, as their energy for activity wanes. Yet it would be wrong for them to feel of little value to society. Rather, they still have a unique part to play. They may have the wisdom of experience to offer, the ripeness of character to show, or memories of warnings or encouragements to share.

Nor need they only look back. Far from curling up in themselves and giving way to self-pity, or worse, to boredom, life can be lived fully in the present. Every new day can be viewed as an exploration into the unknown, with its own sense of adventure. New interest or renewed hobbies can excite fresh creativity, and there is no lack of people, near or far, who will benefit from the kindly word or letter. There are no limits for a love unconditionally offered.

The future also beckons; whether it is long or short matters less than its quality. There is the prospect of life after death to be faced and, if prepared for properly, to be rejoiced in. The promise of the fullness of life, made by the one who pioneers the way on by his resurrection, was not limited to this present life. Old age is a misnomer: full age is better, and the best is yet to come.

P.S. If you think this is irrelevant for you on account of your age, are you helping older folk to end their days happily, and are you preparing yourself for those days?

THE THIRD AGE, AN ARTICLE BY ANDREW SALMON

FURTHER READING

Michael Apichella, *The Church's Hidden Asset*, Kevin Mayhew, 2001.

Albert Jewell (ed.), *Older People and the Church*, Methodist Publishing House, 2001.

Albert Jewell (ed.), *Ageing and Spirituality*, Jessica Kingsley, 1999.

Rob Merchant, *Pioneering the Third Age: The Church in an Ageing Population*, Paternoster Press, 2003.

Guidelines

Magazine

Should I stay or should I go?

Stephen Hance

Ministry can be tough—but that toughness is hard to read. Are the frustration and heartache simply a part of the cost of ministry, or a sign that it's time to move on? After all, even Jesus preached in one town where he could not work effectively, and he told his disciples to shake the dust off their feet when they found a place where their ministry was not welcome.

I write from experience. For nearly five years I have been vicar of a church—Ascension, Balham Hill —which I love leading. I have a strong sense of being in the right place and a desire to stay for a long time. I love the people and believe they love me. In fact, I enjoy leading this church more each year as the things that initially frustrated me are addressed and resolved. Of course there are disappointments and setbacks as well, but I can cope with them in a context where the overall picture is positive.

Before this, I was vicar of a church in north London which felt quite different. Numbers were small. There was no money. Vision for change was not received well. The role of the vicar was to pastor the little congregation, not to stimulate growth. Newcomers were often ignored. There were constant legal battles over a church hall that

had previously been handed over to an independent church group without diocesan permission. The church was part of a team ministry that did not function well. After two years I was signed off sick for a fortnight with stress. Within three years I left.

What makes the difference between the pressures of my former situation and those I face now? How can I tell when it's time to move on? Among other factors—family and health, for example—four stand out to me.

Where you fit

For people called to cross-cultural mission work—and that includes some people in parish ministry— this may look slightly different. But for most of us, there should be a sense of good fit in at least some of the following areas.

Demographics: When I was appointed to my former post I was 30 years old, from a small, wealthy southern city, white, middle-class, with three degrees to my name. My congregation was a largely elderly, working-class, uneducated, retired or unemployed, black inner-London church. That's not insurmountable—but it doesn't make life any easier.

Parish ministry is more likely to work smoothly where there is a demographic overlap between the congregation, the parish and the minister. I'm not saying it can't work otherwise, but there will be additional hurdles to overcome.

Relationships: Linked to this is the question of relationships. Ministry is relational. Our relationships within the church, and the wider team if one exists, can make a difficult situation bearable—or an OK situation untenable.

So it is crucial to ask, can I relate to these people? Do I like them? Do they like me? And if there are other staff, can I work with them? Can we trust each other as colleagues, perhaps become friends?

If the answer to most of these questions is no, it may be time to go.

Gifts: I have always thought of myself as a preacher and teacher. In my curacy—a very happy experience in a south coast church—this was what people appreciated most about my ministry. I believed that it is possible to teach a church into mission and growth.

I still believe this is true in many situations, but not all. I found that preaching and teaching in my former church made little or no difference. A challenging, even confrontational, message would be greeted in precisely the same way as a comforting or bland one.

This came home to me when the Area Dean came to preach. His purpose was to tell the church that unless we started looking outwards and embracing change, we would close. His opening line was 'I will be blunt'—and he was. After the service, only one person spoke to him about what he had said, a long-serving churchwarden who said, 'Lovely sermon—thanks for coming.' I realized that day that preaching was not going to achieve what I had hoped.

Leading a church where your primary gift does not work is like writing a book with your writing hand tied behind your back. If your gift doesn't fit, it's probably time to go.

> *If your gift doesn't fit, it's probably time to go*

Where you can take a step

A lot has been written in recent years about the importance of vision in leadership. We have been reminded by many commentators that a clear and compelling vision of the future is essential for leaders in any type of organization, and I am convinced that all this is true. In my present parish, my first task was to take a group of leaders away for a day to define our vision.

But vision has to be implemented in lots of bite-sized chunks. Drafting the vision statement is the easy bit—and my former parish had done this. Breaking it down into feasible steps is much harder, and sometimes you cannot see a single realistic next step to take.

By the end of my time in north London, this was my situation. We had a vision, but no way of putting it into action. We had no money, a crumbling building, few if any leaders, constant legal battles over the hall and a dysfunctional team.

When you reach the point where you cannot see the next step, it may be time to go.

Where you can build a team

Not so long ago, the expectation in the Church of England was that the parish priest did pretty much everything. He was a lone ranger, paid by the parish through their quota to meet their needs. He preached, pastored, visited, and led the Bible study and prayer meeting. If he was married, his wife probably ran the Sunday school.

Times have changed—although whether the people in the pews have fully grasped those changes, in every parish, is another question. Now we're taught to be team builders, to practise collaborative ministry—and I fully endorse the new thinking. Why are teams so vital?

Because none of us can do it all: Clergy are not omni-competent. The gifted preacher may be a poor pastor. The great visionary may be a mediocre strategist. None of us can meet all the demands that increasingly complex parishes and congregations make upon us.

Because we need support: The lone ranger is a lonely vicar. Without a team we easily become isolated, disappointed, frustrated and angry. As we minister to others, we need others who can minister to us.

Because Jesus taught us to: If anyone had what it took to be a lone ranger, Jesus did. Yet he surrounded himself with others, and invested heavily in them. The New Testament makes it clear that the early Church was team-led.

Not every church will have a ministry team in place. But what if, after a period of time, it becomes obvious that no team can be formed? One strategy is to pray that God will send people who can become a ministry team with you. But if God doesn't answer that prayer, and the one-man or one-woman model of ministry appears to be the only option if you stay, it may be time to go.

Where you are called

The issue of how we discern calling merits an article of its own, and the factors already mentioned will be part of how we weigh up whether God has called us to a particular situation. But there is also a more subjective sense of calling that many ministers experience.

In my former parish, the issues I have talked about were clearly problems within weeks or months of beginning ministry there, yet I stayed for nearly three years. It was not that I didn't think about leaving or scan the job ads in the church press wistfully—I did, and often I longed to leave. But I did nothing about it, because I had a sense that God had called me there.

That changed while I was away at a clergy conference. Before leaving for the conference, the pressure had built to an almost unbearable level. I had begun looking at job ads again, with a bit more interest this time. Yet still I wondered if God wanted me to stay put.

Then, during a time of worship, I felt a physical sensation as if a heavy burden was being lifted from my shoulders, and heard a whisper that seemed to come from the Holy Spirit, which said, 'You're free to go.' After that conference session I telephoned my wife, Jacqui, and told her what had happened. We agreed that God had released us from the calling we had felt, and it was time to go. Four months later I was appointed to my present post.

We announced to an astonished congregation that we were on our way, and ten months after that experience I was inducted as Vicar of Ascension, Balham Hill. I will stay here until the sense of calling I feel now leaves me.

I imagine that some reading this will have been in situations such as the one I describe for much longer than I was, or may have gone from one parish like that to another one. Some might feel that three years was not long enough to fully explore the possibilities, or that I am lucky to have found a parish where I feel so much at home now, when some clergy never do. There may be truth in these points of view. But it is also true that, while some ministers may cut and run too soon, there are many more who keep struggling on wearily, year after year, when all vision has gone, morale is low, hope has died and the only goal is to survive. I don't believe this is what God has in mind for those who have obeyed his call to serve him in church leadership.

Stephen Hance is Vicar of The Ascension Balham Hill, in Southwark Diocese, and Director for Post-Ordination Training in Kingston Episcopal Area. He is also Chair of Just 10 South London, and the author of Beyond Confirmation *(BRF, 2003) and (with his wife, Jacqui)* In The Beginning *(BRF, 2000).*

Barnabas and Godly Play

Lucy Moore

The group of children had been delightfully loud and had thrown themselves into the games with the energy that only the very young can muster late on a Saturday afternoon. But now they were silent and completely focused on the brightly coloured objects in front of them—a strip of dark blue felt and, lying on it, shiny gold stars, a burning nightlight, deep green trees, a delicate white feather, tiny animals and people…

I sat back and looked up.

'I wonder… I wonder what you liked best about this story?'

The replies came, tentative at first, then more confident: 'The water!' 'The animals!' The children went on voicing what they thought, listening to each other but firm in their own opinions.

We moved on: 'I wonder which part of this story is most important?'

'The light!'

'Hmmm, do you mean the light at the start of the story or the light when the sun and moon and stars were made?'

'At the start, because you need that light before anything else can happen.'

'No, water's most important because everything needs water to grow—look—all of it, plants and that, fishes, animals, us…'

'The whole story is the most important. You need all of it together. It all needs each other.'

'God's most important.'

'But you can't see God in the story!'

'But you know he's there or there'd be nothing there at all…'

And the questions moved the children on again: 'I wonder if there's anything we could leave out and still have all the story we need?' 'I wonder which part of this story is most about you?'

I packed away the pieces of the story into their box and we enjoyed for a moment the sense of having been on a journey of discovery together.

This approach to storytelling is based on the style known as 'Godly Play'. But it's more than just storytelling. Through its measured pace, the creation of 'sacred space', its invitation to open-ended response and the reverence with which both stories and listeners are treated, it draws listeners in not only to enjoy a story but to respond and worship the God who plays such a major part in it. It's becoming very popular in the UK as children's leaders discover the excitement of giving children an opportunity to enter deeply into scripture, to explore it on their own terms and to discover a language in which to respond to God.

The idea of Godly Play comes from an Episcopal minister in the States, Jerome Berryman, who has been working on the scheme for over 20 years. Influenced by Maria Montessori's work with children, Berryman has developed the work into a fully scripted year's programme.

Here at BRF we've found ourselves drawn to Godly Play because of the way it encompasses respect for scripture and for the spirituality of children. Godly Play is moving into aspects of our children's work in schools and churches, and into our work with adults too, as we use this approach to opening up scripture with children's leaders. At a recent Quiet Day in Guildford Diocese, the feedback forms showed how powerful and moving listeners had found the stories.

As well as leading Godly Play sessions ourselves with children, we are called on to offer introductions to Godly Play to people thinking about the approach or wanting to take it one step further. It is a privilege and thrill to see how much people enjoy it and benefit from it.

I was storytelling in a school in Worthing and had decided to try the Godly Play story about the Good Shepherd. I wondered if the class of children with special needs were going to cope with the request to be still for a good 20 minutes, but, although one child had to be removed beforehand, the rest of the class were gripped. It was particularly moving to hear their experiences of the 'dark and dangerous places' where the sheep in the story got lost and needed to be rescued.

The same story worked just as powerfully with an aged Mothers' Union group, some of whom were moved to tears. The Creation story, used with a group of teenagers, provoked a fiery discussion about God's goodness, to the astonishment of two non-churchgoing girls who had thought they were just coming to the workshop for a bit of a laugh.

There is a great deal of emphasis in Godly Play on 'sacred space'—the space in which the stories are told, the space within the stories and the space to respond creatively to what is discovered. These quiet, reflective, deceptively simple stories give us an opportunity to create sacred space in the lives of children and adults, space that gives God a chance to speak to us all through his word.

If you'd like to support our Barnabas children's ministry, please use the response form on page 156.

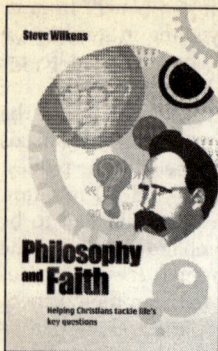

An extract from
Philosophy and Faith

'Are beliefs worth living and dying for?' 'Is a just society possible?' 'Is God responsible for evil?' These are some of the issues explored in *Philosophy and Faith*, which presents an accessible introduction to the thinking of ten major philosophers from Socrates to Sartre. Author Steve Wilkens shows how getting acquainted with the some of the fundamentals of philosophy can transform our thinking as Christians. Featured here is an abridged extract from the chapter on the 19th-century Danish philosopher Kierkegaard.

Are faith and ethics related?

… When (Kierkegaard) examined the comfortable social conformity and clear rational theology of Danish Lutheranism, he saw little connection between what they called faith and the fear and trembling of an Abraham with the knife wielded above his son Isaac's body. Surely Abraham's faith was something different.

This is the point of Kierkegaard's *Fear and Trembling*; Danish Lutheranism had removed the anguish and terror from faith and turned it into a mass-marketed commodity that anyone could be comfortable with. Since faith is the one precondition of Christianity, the Danish church, which replaced the full-bodied faith of an Abraham with a faded image, could not be called Christian. Instead, Kierkegaard refers to it as 'Christendom', the institutional shadow of real Christianity that finds solace in moral and social respectability…

From Kierkegaard's perspective, Christendom's perversion of faith had a willing philosophical accomplice in the ideas of G.W.F. Hegel (1770–1831)… Hegel argues that to get the clearest picture of the Absolute, which is rational in nature, requires that we employ reason. In other words, philosophy, with its anchor wedged into rationality, gives us a better handle on the divine than theology, which combines the reasonable with irrational elements. Thus, for Hegel, faith is a step on the road to reason, which is the more coherent means of expressing reality.

Kierkegaard believed that Hegel had so influenced Danish Lutheranism that the latter gave the impression that salvation is found in the fulfilment of social obligations.

Christianity is transformed into something logical, orderly and systematic—something devoid of passion. When we fulfil moral duties to fellow citizens, the demands of the Absolute are satisfied…

Abraham's journey of faith

…*Fear and Trembling* opens with a series of attempts to make Abraham's call to sacrifice Isaac comprehensible to reason. We could understand Abraham if he made himself appear demented to Isaac… Abraham might have protected himself psychologically by concluding that he had loved Isaac too much and that God's command was a means of rearranging his priorities. We might make sense of Abraham if he dutifully goes through the motions with doubt and hesitation, but nonetheless resigns himself to his awful, God-given task. The problem is that these scenarios, although they make Abraham's actions coherent and rationally defensible, are not true to the biblical account…

Three *Problemata*

…Kierkegaard now builds on his earlier distinction between faith and ethics… by outlining more specific differences in three *Problemata*. All three *Problemata* begin by identifying a basic element of Hegel's ethical philosophy… Kierkegaard then shows how Abraham's actions fail to meet the requirements of ethics… By breaking matters down to these three ethical principles,

Kierkegaard wants Danish Christendom to recognize that faith is not an aspect of ethics, but something radically distinct.

…In Hegel's view, ethics is always social. What is good benefits the whole of humanity… Reason tells us that Abraham's social duty is to protect his son and that Isaac embodies the hope that Abraham's descendants will bless the entire world. But Abraham is quite prepared to kill him despite the fact that humanity will be harmed by his death… When confronted with a choice between moral responsibility and his relationship with God, he determines that the latter is the higher goal, and thus his ethical obligations are suspended…

(There is) a fundamental difference between Hegel and Kierkegaard concerning salvation. For Hegel, the Absolute is awesome by reason of its scope. All reality is eventually swallowed in a single gulp of salvation. This social dimension of salvation makes it a fearful matter for the Hegelian to be isolated from society. For Kierkegaard, however… salvation requires that we separate ourselves from the herd and stand alone before the Wholly Other God. This is exactly where Abraham found himself—isolated from society and incapable of being comprehended by others…

For the Hegelian… ethical individuals have an obligation to explain their actions. Ethical explanation is possible because the universal is logical and orderly… But

God's mind does not conform to human canons of rationality… What Abraham cannot do, given the limitations of our mind to comprehend God's ways, is explain why God would order him to kill his only son…

Faith as an absurd paradox

The conclusion Kierkegaard intends for us to draw from the comparison of Abraham's actions to the demands of the universal [the Hegelian idea that ethical principles apply to all people at all times] is this: faith is absurd. We must be very careful to understand what he means by absurdity, however. Kierkegaard does not mean that Christianity is untrue. Instead, absurdity means that Christianity does not fit within the parameters of human logic…

Kierkegaard believes that knowing God requires a 'leap of faith'. It is as if we are standing on the edge of a cliff peering into complete darkness. A voice calls out to us: 'Jump and I'll catch you.' … The leap of faith cannot be made on the basis of reason, and there are no halfway measures. This is what Kierkegaard says that faith is—a passionate commitment of our whole being. Only passion can take us where logic cannot go. We can see from this, then, that Kierkegaard's definition of faith is a radical departure from the comfortable, logical and socially acceptable life of Christendom. Christendom is safe; faith requires that we bet everything we have on something that is absurd and out of our control. But why not? Isn't our attempt at control what leaves us in frustration?

Dissecting Kierkegaard

…People in the Christian circles with which I am most familiar tend to be very comfortable in saying that there is much about God and his ways that are mysterious. If God is who scripture says, why would we think that our knowledge of him could be squeezed into neat categories accessible to human logic? At the same time, these Christians would be very reluctant to describe God's ways as absurd. Instead, they would say that there is evidence (if not proof) of God's existence, the deity of Jesus, the reliability of scripture and other foundational Christian beliefs. Since we can reasonably move from these foundations to faith, we do not believe in an absurdity. Kierkegaard's argument is that we cannot have it both ways… Either we rely on faith or we rely on reason. Any attempt to build from reason to faith represents trust in our abilities for salvation, and results in the creation of a finite god that is easy to follow, such as the god of Christendom. The question Kierkegaard raises is whether this is an either–or situation. If reason represents a detour on our journey of faith, is any attempt to establish the validity of faith on rational grounds a deficiency of faith? On the other hand, Kierkegaard would ask how, if God is Wholly Other, our minds can be of any use in establishing a relationship with him.

Similar tensions arise for many Christians in working through Kierkegaard's understanding of salvation and ethics. Many Christians appreciate his warning that we should not equate a moral life with salvation… The difficulty for many, however, is in believing that God would require unethical actions… If the worlds of ethics and salvation are really so different, why does scripture have so much to say about ethical expectations for saved people? However, Kierkegaard would remind us that this same Bible contains the story of Abraham. If his analysis of the call to sacrifice Isaac in *Fear and Trembling* is even close to correct, Kierkegaard makes it difficult to see Abraham as a model of morality.

One of Kierkegaard's most strident criticisms of Christendom was that, in its desire to make God accessible, it waters down the biblical portrayal of God and makes faith easy. I suspect he would also accuse Western Christianity today of the same thing. We package God in a way that minimizes the demands made on those who follow him. There are, to be sure, some requirements. We are expected to avoid actions that would harm others and ourselves. Rules like those in the Ten Commandments are seen as guidelines for proper behaviour. In short, we are counted on to be good people, the type of people that Hegel likes. However, Kierkegaard would say that we cannot define a moral lifestyle as faith if we compare it to the anguish of Abraham. The God who demands the sacrifice of Isaac is a far cry from the friendly, predictable and minimally intrusive portrayal of God so often offered today. To be sure, Kierkegaard argues that Abraham's anguished faith results in his salvation, so the story ultimately ends with a gracious God who is known by Abraham. Nonetheless, many wonder whether Kierkegaard's reading of this story reveals a God of grace and love or a capricious despot who plays games with us…

One of the most disturbing things about *Fear and Trembling* is what happens to our future attempts to read Abraham and Isaac's story. It now may be very difficult to hear it as an inspiring morality play. Morality stories call us to imitation. Surely we are not called to imitate Abraham's intent to sacrifice his son, and Kierkegaard clearly indicates that this is not his message… Abraham is simply a witness to how we should respond when God calls us away from the demands of everyday life, suspends our ethical obligations and requires an illogical leap of faith. If anticipation of this call gives rise to fear and trembling, Kierkegaard might say that you are on your way to faith.

If you would like to order a copy of this book, please turn to page 159.

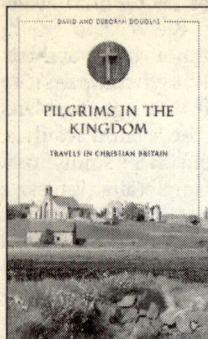

Recommended reading

Pilgrims in the Kingdom by David and Deborah Douglas

The difference between a 'traveller' and a 'tourist' is a perennial topic of debate. Travellers feel that theirs is a more authentic experience, that they take a trip not only to gain understanding of the place visited but also to learn more about themselves. Rather than simply ticking off a list of 'must-see sights' on a whistle-stop tour, they tend to believe that the journey can be as important as the destination. A traveller seeks adventure of one kind or another, and the unexpected is (almost always) welcome.

These days, however, we have multiplying budget airlines, packaged 'authentic encounters', and increasingly extreme adventure holidays. Most paths feel well trodden, even in hitherto remote areas, and the chance for true exploration seems confined to those traversing the Himalayas on a skateboard or floating down the Amazon on an airbed.

Pilgrims are the quintessential travellers. Pilgrims set out in search of wonder, seeking to encounter God in some new way, but that encounter does not necessarily involve travelling far from home. Indeed, while Jerusalem, Rome and Compostela top any list of famous pilgrimage destinations, it is all too easy to forget the many holy sites in Britain.

In recent years, the growing interest in Britain's Celtic Christian heritage has brought greater prominence to places such as Iona and Lindisfarne. T.S. Eliot's many fans will be familiar with the name, if not the location, of Little Gidding, but where is George Herbert's Bemerton? What is the Christian connection with Pendle Hill, better known for stories of 17th-century witches? And where exactly in London did John Wesley feel his heart 'strangely warmed'?

Subtitled 'Travels in Christian Britain', *Pilgrims in the Kingdom* explores a personal selection of holy sites in Scotland, England and Wales. Authors David and Deborah Douglas write with a depth of knowledge and appreciation that bring the 16 locations as vividly to life as do the evocative black-and-white photographs that preface each chapter.

Criss-crossing the country, seeking out chapels and sea caves, mountains and cathedrals, retreat centres and holy islands, they show how Britain provides a breadth of Christian landscape perhaps unsurpassed in the world. Some places are well known, the destinations of ancient pilgrimage routes. Others are seldom visited nowadays, yet still identified with particular men and women of bold faith and witness.

Although David and Deborah are in fact based in Arizona, USA, they began researching the book during a two-year stay in St Andrew's, Scotland, and continued their work on subsequent shorter visits. Their perspective as relative outsiders enables them to bring to vivid life settings that might be overlooked by more local visitors.

As well as describing their own pilgrim experience of each place visited, and retelling relevant episodes from history, the authors show how the different sites illustrate different facets of the Christian faith. Whithorn, in southern Scotland, for example, is linked to the fifth-century life of St Ninian. His missionary work among the local pagan tribes is a reminder of the importance of witness in unfavourable circumstances. Canterbury Cathedral speaks of martyrdom in the present era as well as in centuries past, with its chapel dedicated to modern-day figures persecuted and put to death for their faith.

On the lighter side, the authors recount their 'traveller's tales' of when events do not go to plan. David spends hours on a fruitless search for the actual summit of Pendle Hill, while Deborah categorically fails to gain admittance to C.S. Lewis' Oxford college.

The book is designed both for those who will want to dig out the road atlas and start planning their own trips and for armchair pilgrims who simply want to be reminded (or to learn for the first time) about these places. A concluding section of travel notes provides contact details, access information and also suggestions for further reading linked to each site.

Running throughout the chapters is the concept of the 'thin place'—a place where God seems somehow closer, more accessible to the seeker—and it is this sense of the nearness of eternity that the authors stumble across again and again. What is more, the book opens readers to the possibility of finding their own 'thin places' as well as visiting those described here. This is encapsulated in a quote from Evelyn Underhill, which the authors include in their introduction: '...to the eyes of worship, the whole of the visible world, even its most unlikely patches, is rather thin'.

If you would like to order a copy of this book, please turn to page 159.

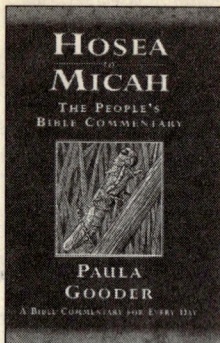

The People's Bible Commentary

HOSEA
to
MICAH
THE PEOPLE'S
BIBLE COMMENTARY

PAULA
GOODER
A BIBLE COMMENTARY FOR EVERY DAY

The six prophetic books that run from Hosea to Micah range from the well-known prophetic writings of Hosea and Amos, to Jonah, a light-hearted story of prophetic disaster, and Obadiah, a book that most people know hardly anything about. Although the texts come from different times, places and prophets, they all tell the story of God's great and abiding love for his people, and also his concern for other nations and how they relate to his plan for history. Author Dr Paula Gooder is a part-time tutor at the Queen's Foundation for Ecumenical Theological Education, Birmingham, and a freelance writer and lecturer on the Bible.

MICAH 5:1–6

YOU, O BETHLEHEM

Generally speaking, the book of Micah is not well known. Most of the prophecies it contains will be new to you. There are bits, however, which are so well known that they almost leap off the page at us. This passage is one of them—known not in this context but in the context of the Christmas story. Micah 5:2 is the verse cited in Matthew 2:6 by Herod's scribes when Herod enquired about the birthplace of the Messiah. Consequently this passage is regularly read out at Christmas as one of the passages of Old Testament background to Jesus' birth narrative. Passages that we

know as well as this pose something of a challenge to us. It is hard to read it in its current context and in its own right, rather than solely in the light of the context in which we know it best. Nevertheless it is important to try. Passages such as this function at different levels. It is right and good to interpret them in the light of Christ but we also need to acknowledge that they had a life before the birth of Christ. If we can gain some insights into what they meant to people before Christ was born, it might help us to understand more about what they are telling us about Christ.

From helpless leader to powerful ruler

In verse 1, Micah seems to be describing the helplessness of the current leader. He is 'walled around with a wall' and struck upon the cheek during a siege. In contrast to this, a new ruler will come forth who will nurture his flock in the strength of God and ensure the security of the land (5:4)... The current problem of Judah is that the leaders are self-interested and impotent but Micah looks forward to a time when a leader will be born who will rule as God would, with compassion for his people (like a shepherd) and with strength (to keep them safe). Micah's vision is, therefore, a concrete one, which focuses the hope of the people on to a future ruler who will keep them safe, standing in contrast to the current leader who provides none of this.

One of the features of this leader is that he will come from 'one of the little clans of Judah' (5:2)... The new ruler would be nothing like the current rulers of Judah but would, like their very first king, come from humble origins. Judah desperately needs a new start. As we noticed in the previous passage, this new start will take place after the labour pains that Judah is currently experiencing. Just as it will be like a new exodus, their ruler will be a new David. Their future will be like all the glorious events of the past rolled into one.

Jesus as the new ruler

The reason why this passage becomes so appropriately applied to Jesus is because this longed-for ruler never came... The people of Judah were left wondering when this hope would become reality. Christians believe that these hopes became a reality with Jesus' birth, life, death and resurrection. Thus these passages become appropriately applied to Jesus. What comes as a surprise, however, is how much Jesus subverts these expectations as well as fulfilling them. The people hoped for a king with humble origins like David but never dreamed that the origins would be as humble as the birth he actually had. They hoped that he would come from a small place like Bethlehem, but not that he would, throughout his ministry, focus on the small, unglamorous aspects of life. Christians believe that Jesus was the longed-for ruler but, in being so, blew apart all previous expectations of what he would be like. These prophetic passages pointed towards him but he surpassed them in ways that no one could have expected.

Prayer

Loving God, you pointed us towards the coming of your son, Jesus Christ, but then surprised us by his fulfilment of your promises. Give us the ability to live in constant expectation of surprise as, each day, we learn more about him.

For reflection:
Centuries of Meditation

Eternity is a mysterious absence of times and ages: an endless length of ages always present, and for ever perfect. For as there is an immovable space wherein all finite spaces are enclosed, and all motions carried on and performed; so is there an immovable duration, that contains and measures all moving durations... the infinite immovable duration is Eternity, the place and duration of all things, even of infinite space itself: the cause and end, the author and beautifier, the life and perfection of all.

Eternity magnifies our joys exceedingly, for whereas things in themselves began, and quickly end; before they came, were never in being; do service but for few moments; and after they are gone pass away and leave us for ever, Eternity retains the moments of their beginning and ending within itself: and from everlasting to everlasting those things were in their times and places before God, and in all their circumstances eternally will be, serving Him in those moments wherein they existed, to those intents and purposes for which they were created. The swiftest thought is present with Him eternally: the creation and the day of judgment, His first consultation, choice and determination, the result and end of all just now in full perfection, ever beginning, ever passing, ever ending with all the intervals of space between things and things: As if those objects that arise many thousand years one after the other were all together. We also were ourselves before God eternally; and have the joy of seeing ourselves eternally beloved and eternally blessed, and infinitely enjoying all the parts of our blessedness; in all the durations of eternity appearing at once before ourselves, when perfectly consummate in the Kingdom of Light and Glory. The smallest thing by the influence of eternity, is made infinite and eternal. We pass through a standing continent or region of ages, that are already before us, glorious and perfect while we come to them. Like men in a ship we pass forward, the shores and marks seeming to go backward, though we move and they stand still. We are not with them in our progressive motion, but prevent the swiftness of our course, and are present with them in our understandings. Like the sun we dart our rays before us, and occupy those spaces with light and contemplation which we move towards, but possess not with our bodies. And seeing all things in the light of Divine knowledge, eternally serving God, rejoice unspeakably in that service, and enjoy it all.

His omnipresence is our ample territory or field of joys, a transparent temple of infinite lustre, a strong tower of defence, a castle of repose, a bulwark of security, a palace of delights, an immediate help, and a present refuge in the needful time of trouble, a broad and a vast extent of fame and glory, a theatre of infinite excellency, an infinite ocean by means whereof every action, word, and thought is immediately diffused like a drop of wine in a pail of water, and everywhere present, everywhere seen and known, infinitely delighted in, as well as filling infinite spaces. It is the Spirit that pervades all His works, the life and soul of the universe, that in every point of space from the centre to the heavens, in every kingdom in the world, in every city, in every wilderness, in every house, every soul, every creature, in all the parts of His infinity and eternity sees our persons; loves our virtues, inspires us with itself, and crowns our actions with praise and glory. It makes our honour infinite in extent, our glory immense, and our happiness eternal. The rays of our light are by this means darted

> *It is the Spirit that pervades all His works*

from everlasting to everlasting. This spiritual region makes us infinitely present with God, Angels, and Men in all places from the utmost bounds of the everlasting hills, throughout all the unwearied durations of His endless infinity, and gives us the sense and feeling of all the delights and praises we occasion, as well as of all the beauties and powers, and pleasures and glories which God enjoyeth or createth.

Our Bridegroom and our King being everywhere, our Lover and Defender watchfully governing all worlds, no danger or enemy can arise to hurt us, but is immediately prevented and suppressed, in all the spaces beyond the utmost borders of those unknown habitations which He possesseth. Delights of inestimable value are there preparing, for everything is present by its own existence. The essence of God therefore being all light and knowledge, love and goodness, care and providence, felicity and glory, a pure and simple act, it is present in its operations, and by those acts which it eternally exerteth is wholly busied in all parts and places of His dominion, perfecting and completing our bliss and happiness.

Thomas Traherne (?1636–1674), from the Fifth Century, *Centuries of Meditation*

Guidelines © BRF 2005

The Bible Reading Fellowship
First Floor, Elsfield Hall, 15–17 Elsfield Way, Oxford OX2 8FG
Tel: 01865 319700; Fax: 01865 319701
E-mail: enquiries@brf.org.uk
Website: www.brf.org.uk

ISBN 1 84101 292 0

Distributed in Australia by:
Willow Connection, PO Box 288, Brookvale, NSW 2100.
Tel: 02 9948 3957; Fax: 02 9948 8153;
E-mail: info@willowconnection.com.au
Available also from all good Christian bookshops in Australia.
For individual and group subscriptions in Australia:
Mrs Rosemary Morrall, PO Box W35, Wanniassa, ACT 2903.

Distributed in New Zealand by:
Scripture Union Wholesale, PO Box 760, Wellington
Tel: 04 385 0421; Fax: 04 384 3990; E-mail: suwholesale@clear.net.nz

Publications distributed to more than 60 countries

Acknowledgments
The New Revised Standard Version of the Bible, Anglicized Edition, copyright © 1989,
1995 by the Division of Christian Education of the National Council of the Churches
of Christ in the USA. Used by permission. All rights reserved.

The Holy Bible, New International Version, copyright © 1973, 1978, 1984 by
International Bible Society. Used by permission of Hodder & Stoughton Limited. All
rights reserved. 'NIV' is a registered trademark of International Bible Society. UK
trademark number 1448790.

Printed in Denmark

BRF is a Christian charity committed to resourcing the spiritual journey of adults and children alike. For adults, BRF publishes Bible reading notes and books and offers an annual programme of quiet days and retreats. Under its children's imprint *Barnabas*, BRF publishes a wide range of books for those working with children under 11 in school, church and home. BRF's *Barnabas Ministry* team offers INSET sessions for primary teachers, training for children's leaders in church, quiet days, and a range of events to enable children themselves to engage with the Bible and its message.

We need your help if we are to make a real impact on the local church and community. In an increasingly secular world people need even more help with their Bible reading, their prayer and their discipleship. We can do something about this, but our resources are limited. With your help, if we all do a little, together we can make a huge difference.

How can you help?

- You could support BRF's ministry with a donation or standing order (using the response form overleaf).

- You could consider making a bequest to BRF in your will, and so give lasting support to our work. (We have a leaflet available with more information about this, which can be requested using the form overleaf.)

- And, most important of all, you could support BRF with your prayers.

Whatever you can do or give, we thank you for your support.

BRF – resourcing your spiritual journey

BRF MINISTRY APPEAL RESPONSE FORM

Name _____

Address _____

_____ Postcode _____

Telephone _____ Email _____

(tick as appropriate)

Gift Aid Declaration

☐ I am a UK taxpayer. I want BRF to treat as Gift Aid Donations all donations I make from 6 April 2000 until I notify you otherwise.

Signature _____ Date _____

☐ I would like to support BRF's ministry with a regular donation by standing order (please complete the Banker's Order below).

Standing Order – Banker's Order

To the Manager, Name of Bank/Building Society _____

Address _____

_____ Postcode _____

Sort Code _____ Account Name _____

Account No _____

Please pay Royal Bank of Scotland plc, London Drummonds Branch, 49 Charing Cross, London SW1A 2DX (Sort Code 16-00-38), for the account of BRF A/C No. 00774151

The sum of _____ pounds on ___ /___ /___ (insert date your standing order starts) and thereafter the same amount on the same day of each month until further notice.

Signature _____ Date _____

Single donation

☐ I enclose my cheque/credit card/Switch card details for a donation of £5 £10 £25 £50 £100 £250 (other) £ _____ to support BRF's ministry

Credit/ Switch card no. ☐☐☐☐☐☐☐☐☐☐☐☐☐☐☐☐☐☐☐

Expires ☐☐ ☐☐   Issue no. of Switch card ☐☐☐

Signature _____ Date _____

(Where appropriate, on receipt of your donation, we will send you a Gift Aid form)

☐ Please send me information about making a bequest to BRF in my will.

Please detach and send this completed form to: Richard Fisher, BRF, First Floor, Elsfield Hall, 15–17 Elsfield Way, Oxford OX2 8FG. BRF is a Registered Charity (No.233280)

GUIDELINES SUBSCRIPTIONS

Please note our subscription rates 2005–2006. From the May 2005 issue, the new subscription rates will be:

Individual subscriptions covering 3 issues for under 5 copies, payable in advance (including postage and packing):

		UK	SURFACE	AIRMAIL
GUIDELINES each set of 3 p.a.		£11.70	£13.05	£15.30
GUIDELINES 3-year sub	i.e. 9 issues	£29.25	N/A	N/A

Group subscriptions covering 3 issues for 5 copies or more, sent to ONE address (post free):

GUIDELINES	£9.75	each set of 3 p.a.

Please note that the annual billing period for Group Subscriptions runs from 1 May to 30 April.

Copies of the notes may also be obtained from Christian bookshops:

GUIDELINES	£3.25 each copy

GUIDELINES SUBSCRIPTIONS

❏ I would like to give a gift subscription (please complete both name and address sections below)

❏ I would like to take out a subscription myself (complete name and address details only once)

This completed coupon should be sent with appropriate payment to BRF. Alternatively, please write to us quoting your name, address, the subscription you would like for either yourself or a friend (with their name and address), the start date and credit card number, expiry date and signature if paying by credit card.

Gift subscription name _____

Gift subscription address_____

_____Postcode _____

Please send beginning with the May / September 2005 / January 2006 issue: (delete as applicable)

(please tick box)	UK	SURFACE	AIR MAIL
GUIDELINES	❏ £11.70	❏ £13.05	❏ £15.30
GUIDELINES 3-year sub	❏ £29.25		

Please complete the payment details below and send your coupon, with appropriate payment to: **BRF, First Floor, Elsfield Hall, 15–17 Elsfield Way, Oxford OX2 8FG.**

Your name _____

Your address_____

_____Postcode _____

Total enclosed £ _____ (cheques should be made payable to 'BRF')

Payment by cheque ❏ postal order ❏ Visa ❏ Mastercard ❏ Switch ❏

Card number: ⬚⬚⬚⬚⬚⬚⬚⬚⬚⬚⬚⬚⬚⬚⬚⬚

Expiry date of card: ⬚⬚⬚⬚ Issue number (Switch): ⬚⬚⬚⬚

Signature (essential if paying by credit/Switch card)_____

❏ Please do not send me further information about BRF publications.

BRF is a Registered Charity

BRF PUBLICATIONS ORDER FORM

Please ensure that you complete and send off both sides of this order form.

Please send me the following book(s):

		Quantity	Price	Total
241 6	Beyond Confirmation *(S. Hance)*	_____	£6.99	_____
324 2	Philosophy and Faith *(S. Wilkens)*	_____	£12.99	_____
365 X	Challenges of the Narrow Way *(B. Plass)*	_____	£7.99	_____
225 4	Pilgrims in the Kingdom *(D. & D. Douglas)*	_____	£12.99	_____
264 5	A-cross the World *(M. Payne & B. Pedley)*	_____	£15.99	_____
192 4	PBC: Leviticus and Numbers *(M. Butterworth)*	_____	£7.99	_____
095 2	PBC: Joshua and Judges *(S. Mathewson)*	_____	£7.99	_____
242 4	PBC: Ruth, Esther, Ecclesiastes, Song, Lamentations *(R. Fyall)*	_____	£8.99	_____
030 8	PBC: 1 & 2 Samuel *(H. Mowvley)*	_____	£7.99	_____
118 5	PBC: 1 & 2 Kings *(S. Dawes)*	_____	£7.99	_____
070 7	PBC: Chronicles—Nehemiah *(M. Tunnicliffe)*	_____	£7.99	_____
094 4	PBC: Job *(K. Dell)*	_____	£7.99	_____
065 0	PBC: Psalms 73—150 *(D. Coggan)*	_____	£7.99	_____
071 5	PBC: Proverbs *(E. Mellor)*	_____	£7.99	_____
087 1	PBC: Jeremiah *(R. Mason)*	_____	£7.99	_____
040 5	PBC: Ezekiel *(E. Lucas)*	_____	£7.99	_____
245 9	PBC: Hosea—Micah *(P. Gooder)* (NEW)	_____	£8.99	_____
028 6	PBC: Nahum—Malachi *(G. Emmerson)*	_____	£7.99	_____
191 6	PBC: Matthew *(J. Proctor)*	_____	£7.99	_____
046 4	PBC: Mark *(D. France)*	_____	£8.99	_____
027 8	PBC: Luke *(H. Wansbrough)*	_____	£7.99	_____
029 4	PBC: John *(R.A. Burridge)*	_____	£7.99	_____
082 0	PBC: Romans *(J. Dunn)*	_____	£7.99	_____
122 3	PBC: 1 Corinthians *(J. Murphy-O'Connor)*	_____	£7.99	_____
073 1	PBC: 2 Corinthians *(A. Besançon Spencer)*	_____	£7.99	_____
012 X	PBC: Galatians and 1 & 2 Thessalonians *(J. Fenton)*	_____	£7.99	_____
047 2	PBC: Ephesians—Colossians & Philemon *(M. Maxwell)*	_____	£7.99	_____
119 3	PBC: Timothy, Titus and Hebrews *(D. France)*	_____	£7.99	_____
092 8	PBC: James—Jude *(F. Moloney)*	_____	£7.99	_____

Total cost of books £ _____

Postage and packing (see over) £ _____

TOTAL £ _____

See over for payment details. All prices are correct at time of going to press, are subject to the prevailing rate of VAT and may be subject to change without prior warning.

BRF publications are available from Christian bookshops.

The Bible Reading Fellowship is a Registered Charity

PAYMENT DETAILS

Please complete the payment details below and send with appropriate payment and completed order form to:

BRF, First Floor, Elsfield Hall,
15–17 Elsfield Way, Oxford OX2 8FG

Name _____

Address _____

_____

_____ Postcode _____

Telephone _____

Email _____

Total enclosed £ _____(cheques should be made payable to 'BRF')

Payment by cheque ❏ postal order ❏ Visa ❏ Mastercard ❏ Switch ❏

Card number: ☐☐☐☐☐☐☐☐☐☐☐☐☐☐☐☐☐☐☐☐

Expiry date of card: ☐☐☐☐   Issue number (Switch): ☐☐☐☐

Signature (essential if paying by credit/Switch card)_____

ALTERNATIVE WAYS TO ORDER

Christian bookshops: All good Christian bookshops stock BRF publications. For your nearest stockist, please contact BRF.

POSTAGE AND PACKING CHARGES				
order value	UK	Europe	Surface	Air Mail
£7.00 & under	£1.25	£3.00	£3.50	£5.50
£7.01–£30.00	£2.25	£5.50	£6.50	£10.00
Over £30.00	free	prices on request		

Telephone: The BRF office is open between 09.15 and 17.30. To place your order, phone 01865 319700; fax 01865 319701.

Web: Visit www.brf.org.uk

❏ Please do not send me further information about BRF publications.

BRF is a Registered Charity